You Can't Feed Butter to a Cat!

TO LOU "THE DOG MAN"

BEST REGARDS

Tony V.

Dad

☎

Rrriiinnnggg…

You Can't Feed Butter to a Cat!
and other conversations I've had with my Dad

by Tony Vavlas

1701 Press
Akron, Ohio

☎

© 2015 Tony Vavlas

For more information:
1701 Press, Akron, Ohio

Published by 1701 Press, Akron, Ohio
www.1701press.com

Printed and bound in the United States of America
First Printing 2015

ISBN 0-978-9842699-9-0

LCCN 2014957627

design: Dominic Caruso

cover photographs: Shari Summers / Moore Summers Photography
www.facebook.com/mooresummersphoto

For my daughters, Holly and Jessica. Holly, words cannot describe how proud I am of you. You are truly a gift from God, but don't ever get the idea of writing your own book someday. Jessica, your angel wings lift me up every day. I love you both.

☎

Additional Praise for
You Can't Feed Butter to a Cat!

"According to *Readers' Digest* 'Laughter Is The Best Medicine.' Truly life's actual experiences can be the most humorous, especially when family is involved. A doctor of laughter, Anthony, hit squarely on the mark with his stories of his father and son conversations."

—*Mrs. Ruby Peltz, Anthony's Third Grade Teacher*

I'VE ALWAYS BEEN CLOSE TO MY FATHER. I couldn't have asked for better parents if I'd been given the chance to choose them myself. My Dad was always a confident man, at least on the surface. I cannot remember one single instance, as a child, that I felt that Dad was not in control. I thought that he had all of the answers. It wasn't until my Mother passed in 2006 that I got to see another side of my Dad. All of his insecurities and questions in life had been filtered through my Mom. With Mom gone... that job now fell on me. The guy that I always went to for answers and advice, was now asking me for advice. I wasn't ready for that. I began writing down the conversations that we had and posted a few of the humorous ones on Facebook, hoping that others would chime in and offer support because they were going through the same thing with their parents. The support that I sought came in the form of messages from folks telling me just how much my posts about Dad brightened their day. I knew I wasn't alone because so many people could relate to these stories on many different levels. Not surprising. Dad's a likeable guy. There's a little bit of Dad in all of our parents, grandparents, aunts and uncles... and I guess, in all of us as well. Dad and I hope that these stories can continue to brighten your days.

I'd like to thank God for being God. I'd like to thank a few friends who relentlessly badgered me to collect the stories and publish them. Without them, these stories would still merely be Facebook statuses. I would like to especially acknowledge and thank Alaina Greenwood Maloney, Lucille Petsche, Maryellen Derrick, and Joyce Ann Zitkovich for the PUSH that finally moved me to action. Thank you for being "pushy" at times, in my moments of self-doubt. I would also like to thank Shari Summers and Margarita Crow for their technical and creative assistance. I owe you all a debt of gratitude.

I would like to thank my wife Belinda and daughter Holly for all of their love and understanding through this book writing process. Thank you to ALL of my friends and family for their constant support. Thank you to all of you who read, liked and commented on these stories on Facebook. Thank you to Dad for being Dad and making me laugh every day. And lastly, thank you to Mom for all that you did and continue to do for me. XO...

On the day my Mom passed, I had this conversation with Dad...

Me: What are we going to do now?

Dad: We're gonna live... like she wants us to live... like she taught us to live. It's not gonna be easy... but we owe it to her to live and to try to make each other happy... no matter how hard it gets.

I hope that these stories bring you some measure of happiness. If they bring a smile to your face then I've made my Mother proud. May all of your ***Rrriiinnngggs*** be happy ones.

☎
foreword

Me: Hey Dad… The book I've been writing, about you, is done. Well, my part anyways. I think it would be nice if YOU wrote the foreword.

Dad: Just write #$@% and put my name to it.

Me: No Dad, FOREword, not four letter word. It needs to be more than one word, and should be printable.

Dad: What about $#%^&@ %$#^&*… that's two words.

Me: Come on Dad. Be nice. I worked hard on this… can't you just write something nice about the experience of having a book written about you?

Dad: OK… How do you spell slanderous? Never mind… I'll just put LIES!!! All LIES!!!

Me: Even the stories that make you look smart?

Dad: No… Those are true.

Me: Of course.

Dad: Who's gonna buy this book?

Me: Everyone… I hope.

Dad: Hmmmph… Maybe someday it'll be a movie. Who would play me?

Me: Well… Bea Arthur's dead.

Dad: Funny! I'm thinking Al Pacino or Dustin Hoffman.

Me: Well, you are a cross between Tony Montana and Rain Man. Quite a few people have already told me that they want you to autograph a copy of the book for them.

Dad: How did this become work for me? I'm retired.

Me: You should be honored Dad. You are semi-famous.

Dad: Yeah… Thanks for nothing!

~ From games of catch in the yard to trying to find the time to catch up.

~ From bandaging my little scrapes and cuts to some of your very real health scares.

~ From sitting around the dinner table enjoying a great meal that Mom cooked to sitting around the same table trying to figure out what we did wrong even though we used her recipe. RIP Mom.

~ From you dealing out unsolicited advice to me seeking out your advice.

You raised me to be a good kid, and in turn showed me how to be a good Dad. You taught me that you don't have to come from a lot to one day be a lot. From you, I learned that a job well done meant showing up early, staying until the job was done, and giving more than was expected of you. My love of Cleveland sports comes from you and it taught me to be loyal to the bitter end. And there have been plenty of bitter ends. You inspired me, encouraged me, warned me, and picked me up when I had fallen. I never had to look very far to see what it meant to be a good son, a good father and a good man.

We've laughed, we've cried and we've laughed some more. If laughter truly is the best medicine, you should have been a doctor. You could have healed a lot of people. Thank you for everything Dad!

you can't feed butter to a cat

Rrriiinnnggg

Me: Hello.

Dad: How much butter is safe to give a cat?

Me: You can't feed butter to a cat!

Dad: Yes you can. I just did!

Me: I mean, of course you CAN, but you SHOULDN'T! What would possess you to feed butter to your cat?

Dad: Because she wanted some.

Me: How could you possibly know that?

Dad: Because I was eating some and she looked at me at me like she wanted some.

Me: You were eating butter? Why the heck are you eating butter? I'm telling Dr. Frangopoulos.

Dad: I wasn't JUST eating butter. It was on pierogies.

Me: No butter for the cat. Cats don't eat butter.

Dad: *(in a mocking tone)* Cats don't eat butter. Goodbye!

Riiiinnnggg

Me: Hello.

Dad: Can I give my cat margarine?

buy one get one

Rrriiinnnggg

Me: Hello Dad!

Dad: Hey… I bought you an AlumaWallet!

Me: That aluminum wallet from TV?

Dad: Yeah, they were buy one get one.

Me: Great! Just what I need. A wallet the size of a toaster oven.

Dad: The commercial says they protect your valuables.

Me: From what? My leather wallet and pants pocket seem to do an adequate enough job.

Dad: It protects from impact, water spills, drops from high places, x-rays.

Me: Who am I? James Bond? My money doesn't need to be that protected.

Dad: It also has a credit card organizer.

Me: I have one credit card. It stays pretty organized.

Dad: But this one is made out of aluminum.

Me: That just puts me at a higher risk for lightning strikes.

Dad: Shut up!!! Don't ask me to ever buy you anything again!!

Me: I didn't ask you to buy THAT!

Dad: Well, they were buy one get one. So you got one. Just shut up and use it.

Me: Thanks Dad!

(three weeks later)

Rrriiinnnggg

Me: Hello.

Dad: Do you still have that AlumaWallet?

Me: Yes. I haven't used it yet.

Dad: Good. Bring it over. I want it back. Mine broke already.

Tony Vavlas

☎
form fictions

My Dad is going for a sleep study because he was told that he might have sleep apnea. He attempted to fill out his medical forms but quit and called me after two questions.

Rrriiinnnggg

Me: Hello.

Dad: Hey, come over and help me fill out this stupid form.

Me: OK. Be right over.

~ ~ ~ ~ *(I walk to Dad's.)* ~ ~ ~ ~

Me: Under "marital status," you put "whittler." A whittler is someone who carves things out of wood.

Dad: Well why would they need to know that?

Me: Do you mean WIDOWER?

Dad: Probably.

Me: Under "sleep" you answered:
   How much sleep do you get in an average night? — 8½ hours
   How much, on average, do you nap on a daily basis? — 2 hours
10½ hours is more than most people get in two days. Are you SURE you have a sleep problem?

Dad: OK… let's change my answer.

Me: You can't lie.

Dad: Who's gonna know?

coupon

Rrriiinnnggg

Me: Hello!

Dad: I need a favor.

Me: Sure. What is it?

Dad: I need you to go to Neosporin.com and print me out a $2 off coupon for Neosporin.

Me: OK.

(I go to the website and under coupons it says no current offers.)

(I call Dad back.)

Me: Hey Dad I just tried Neosporin.com and they don't currently have any coupons. Where did you hear about it?

Dad: I JUST heard it on a TV commercial.

Me: OK. I'll try again.

(try again—same result—call Dad back)

Me: Hey Dad, I tried again and I can't find any coupons. Are you sure you got the website right? What show are you watching?

Dad: I'm sure... I JUST saw it like three minutes ago.

(I try again, searching the internet for 45 minutes, and looking for Neosporin coupons. No luck—re-call Dad.)

Me: Hey Dad. I can't find a coupon for Neosporin anywhere. Are you positive that you heard that there was a coupon?

Dad: Yeah. Wait, I'll rewind the show to the commercial and listen again.

Me: REWIND???

Dad: Yeah, I found this old show on my DVR and I'm finally watching it. It's a Trans-Siberian Orchestra Christmas special that I never watched during the holidays.

Me: And the commercial was on there? Ten months ago?

Dad: Never mind. I'll just use the coupon from the newspaper.

Me: Do you have any coupons for Excedrin???

Tony Vavlas

49 over 6

Rrriiinnnggg

Me: Hello.

Dad: Hey, I just took my blood pressure and it's 49 over 6.

Me: OK, I will call Wasko's Funeral Home. Do you need a ride or can you drive?

Dad: I think I can drive.

Me: OK. Let me know what they say.

Dad: Seriously, is that bad?

Me: Yes, where did you get the blood pressure monitor?

Dad: At Marc's Discount Store for $14.

Me: Well how do you feel?

Dad: Not so good SINCE I took my blood pressure.

Me: Well, I am pretty sure that reading was wrong!

Dad: But this monitor is brand new!

Me: You shoulda bought the pro model for $16.

Dad: Goodbye!

porn?

Rrriiinnnggg

Dad: Hello?

Me: Hi Dad. I'm going to pick up some corn. Do you want any?

Dad: Porn???

You Can't Feed Butter to a Cat!

Me: No Dad, corn. As in corn on the cob!

Dad: Oh… no then!

the decision

(at 7:15 am one morning, on my only day to sleep in)

Rrriiinnnggg

Me: Hello?

Dad: I'm switching to butter.

Me: OK. Should I break it to the rest of the family or are you keeping it a secret?

Dad: ((((((Silence))))))

Me: Dad…

Dad: Yes?

Me: I'm proud of you Dad. A lot of people wouldn't be so brave!!!

Dad: I would have called you last night but I wanted to sleep on my decision first.

Me: That was smart. That's not a decision you should make without a full night's sleep. I hope to get one someday soon. Right after I change my phone number.

<<<CLICK!!!>>>

the kid

Walking through the lobby of Mountaineer Casino with Dad the other day, we saw a large crowd of older folks lined up at one of the windows.

Tony Vavlas

Me: I wonder what they're giving away there?

Dad: From the looks of this crowd… free oxygen tank refills!

He likes going down there because someone always ends up calling him "kid!"

☎
limited time

Rrriiinnnggg

Me: Good Morning Dad!

Dad: Hey, I just saw a commercial on TV. Popeye's has crawfish. I wanna try 'em!

Me: OK. When do you want to go?

Dad: Now!

Me: Dad, it's 9:30 am.

Dad: The commercial said limited time only.

Me: I'm pretty sure we're gonna be safe at noon.

Dad: What do they taste like?

Me: Kind of like a cross between shrimp and lobster.

Dad: I don't like lobster.

Me: Who doesn't like lobster? OK, then we can just get you a shrimp dinner.

Dad: I'm really not crazy about shrimp either. I'll get chicken.

Me: I thought you wanted crawfish.

Dad: I'm over it now. I'll pick you up in ten minutes.

☎

police scanner

Rrriiinnnggg

Me: Hello.

Dad: Hey! Get on your police scanner and tell them I saw five cars go through the stop sign on 13th Street today.

Me: I can't get on the scanner and tell them anything. It's only to listen.

Dad: You mean you can't talk to them on that thing?

Me: No!!! You thought I had instantaneous communication capabilities with law enforcement? Who do you think I am… Batman?

Dad: Well they should make a device that allows you to talk to the police.

Me: They have one… it's the device in your hand right now.

Dad: No! I mean in an instant… without dialing.

Me: That would be dangerous in your hands. You'd be having them stop out at your house fifteen times a night in the summer. Every time a moth sets off your security light.

Dad: Some of those moths are big. Big enough to handcuff.

seat

Rrriiinnnggg

Me: Hello.

Dad: I'm making cinnamon rolls and on the package it says "push spoon against SEAT." Do I really have to do that?

Tony Vavlas

Me: Yep. It is a vital step. It gets the spoon ready to be pushed against the SEAM.

<<<*CLICK.*>>>

☎
tomato burglar

Rrriiinnnggg... at 7:00 am

Me: Hello.

Dad: Hey! I picked all of the tomatoes in your garden. Come over and get them. There's about forty of them.

Me: OK... I'll get some later. I'm working now. I'll be over at 5.

Rrriiinnnggg... at 12:15 pm

Me: Hello.

Dad: Hey! You coming over for these tomatoes?

Me: Yeah Dad... I'll be over after work at 5.

~ ~ ~ ~ *(I walk to Dad's at 5:15 pm.)* ~ ~ ~ ~

Me: Hey Dad... where are the tomatoes?

Dad: I gave them away. I called you twice and you never showed up. I didn't want them to go to waste.

Me: Both times I told you I was working and I'd be over at 5. Did you give them all away?

Dad: Yes I did. Oh wait... there's one on the counter that I cut already. But take the first slice off... it fell on the ground.

Me: So this morning I had forty tomatoes from my garden, you gave them all away and all that is left is one that fell on the floor?

Dad: There's one that fell in the garden and split that I didn't pick up.

Me: Next year... I'm getting a guard dog for the garden.

415

Rrriiinnnggg

Dad: Hello.

Me: Hey Dad, remember when we had that big windstorm last week and I asked you if you had seen my trash can lid and you said NO?

Dad: I remember. I still haven't seen it.

Me: I found it in your garage today.

Dad: Oh?!? I didn't know that was yours.

Me: Yeah I can see how you wouldn't know that, seeing as how I live at 415 Whipple and there's a big 415 painted on it.

Dad: Well, I guess I can stop trying to figure out whose initials are "sih" then huh?

apple

Dad: I go to the doctor's this week. Remind me to tell him that my stomach has been hurting.

Me: Dad! In the two hours that I have been here, you've had two pounds of pork roast, potatoes, sweet potatoes, cranberry sauce, salad, pumpkin crisp, three cookies, a piece of pie, potato chips, rice pudding, and an apple. Why do you think your stomach hurts?

Dad: I probably shouldn't have had that apple, huh?

crap! part 1

Rrriiinnnggg

Dad: Hello

Me: HAPPY BIRTHDAY DAD! What are you doing?

Dad: Making sloppy joes, fela [stuffed grape leaves], stuffed peppers, and stuffed cabbage!

Me: WHAT?!? Why all at the same time?

Dad: I bought my turkey and I didn't have room for it in the freezer so I had to take out fourteen one-pound packages of ground meat.

Me: OK, so you can eat some of it today but what are you going to do with the rest?

Dad: I figured I'd freeze them and then just reheat some whenever I wanted them. They'll all be premade. Pretty smart, huh?

Me: I thought you said your freezers were full?

Dad: Oh crap!!! Don't cook today. We gotta eat this stuff!

stadium brand

(At a Cleveland Indians game with Dad.)

Me: Dad! What are you doing?

Dad: Putting catsup on my hot dog.

Me: You can't use catsup at an Indians game. You gotta use Stadium Brand Mustard and that's it! You taught me that as a kid.

Dad: Well you better ask for some Stadium Brand Catsup 'cuz this old man wants CATSUP!

garlic wings

Rrriiinnnggg

Me: Hello.

Dad: Hey! I went bowling with my friends tonight.

Me: You're not in jail are you?

Dad: No! But I had some garlic wings and now all I taste is garlic.

Me: Well yeah, that's gonna happen. Brush your teeth.

Dad: I tried that already. And mouthwash.

Me: You sure it was mouthwash this time and not Mr. Clean?

Dad: Yeah… I think.

Me: Well chew some gum or eat a mint.

Dad: All I have are these Breath Savers long lasting three hour mints.

Me: OK. Those should work.

Dad: Well should I only take a half?

Me: Why would you do that?

Dad: Because it's late and I'm not gonna be up for three hours.

Me: It's not medicine Dad. You won't overdose.

Dad: You sure? Come over here and read the package to make sure it's OK.

Me: I'm not coming over there to read a candy package. Trust me, it's OK. The people in your dreams will thank me.

☎
crap! part 2

My cousin Renee and her husband Ron visited my Dad one day. Ron forgot his phone at my Dad's.

Dad: No problem. I have his number. I'll call him.

Me: Sure Dad! That's a great idea. Call him.

Rrriiinnnggg

Dad: Oh crap!!!

Ron later called and said he'd be back to pick up the phone. My Dad wasn't going to be home, so Ron asked him to put it in the mailbox in a plastic bag.

As I was leaving Dad's house...

Dad: Here, put this in my mailbox.

Me: Dad!!! This is YOUR phone!!!

Dad: Oh crap!!!

Me: I'm calling Shady Acres Rest Home in the morning!

repairs

Rrriiinnnggg

Me: Hello.

Dad: Hey, I bought an eyeglass repair kit, can you help me fix my glasses?

Me: Sure, I'll be right over!

(We struggle for about an hour before realizing that the kit does not contain the screw size that we need.)

Dad: Oh well, the kit was only three bucks.

Me: You should probably take the glasses to the doctor to get them fixed. They probably need adjusted anyways. They look kind of bent up.

Dad: Oh... I didn't get them from the doctor. Those are 89 cent glasses from Marc's.

the best

Dad flagged me down as I was leaving for work today and told me he had a cold. He asked me to pick up some cold medicine for him.

Dad: Make sure it treats sore throat, aches, fever, itchy watery eyes, congestion, and runny nose.

Me: OK… Athlete's foot and indigestion too?

Dad: And ask the pharmacist what's best.

(Upon returning with said magical, medical elixir.)

Dad: *(reading the label)* Sore throat, aches, fever, itchy watery eyes, congestion and HEY!!! What about runny nose? This isn't going to stop my runny nose!!! Did you ask the pharmacist? What did he say?

Me: He said that this Robitussin Cold Medicine was the absolute best.

Dad: How can it be the best? It won't stop a runny nose! What about my runny nose? What did he say I should take for that?

Me: Two Kleenex and call him in the morning.

anti-moisture

Rrriiinnnggg

Dad: Hey, come over here quick!

~~~~~ *(I walk to Dad's.)* ~~~~~

Me: What's up?

Dad: I bought a new bottle of aspirin. Look at the size of those things.

Tony Vavlas

Me: That's the anti-moisture capsule Dad!!!

Dad: No wonder I'm always so thirsty.

plastic

Rrriiinnnggg

Me: Hello.

Dad: Hey! Dr. Oz says that you shouldn't heat things in plastic containers in your microwave. Plastic in the microwave is poisonous.

Me: Tell Dr. Oz that the inside of my microwave is made out of plastic.

Dad: Oh yeah… it is. Should we line the inside with ceramic tile?

Me: Absolutely NOT!!!

Dad: Well what should I do?

Me: Stop watching Dr. Oz or I'm calling Dr. Peterson… the psychiatrist.

spelling bee

Rrriiinnnggg

Me: Hello.

Dad: Hey, turn on ABC. The Georgia football game is on and your cousin Kosta Vavlas is playing.

Me: OK, I'll look for him. How do you spell his last name?

Dad: V*A*V*L… you idiot! It's our last name.

<<<*CLICK.*>>>

labels

Dad: Look at all of these address labels people send me for free.

Me: Yeah Dad, that's a lot of address labels.

Dad: What should I do with them? I'll never use all of these. Why don't you take half?

Me: Because they have YOUR address on them.

Dad: Scratch it out and write your address on them.

Me: That's redic— I mean THANKS Dad.

Dad: You're gonna throw those away aren't you?

Me: Ohhhhhh noooooooo!

ice packrat

Helping Dad clean out his upright freezer...

Me: Dad, you have fourteen ice packs from doctors and surgery centers. Can we throw thirteen of these away?

Dad: What if I need them?

Me: You have enough here to treat everyone wounded in the Civil War!

Dad: You never know when you might need an ice pack.

Me: It didn't take this much ice to freeze Walt Disney. Have you used these since you put them in the freezer?

Dad: No, but that's because they're downstairs and when I'm sore and need an ice pack I don't feel like coming down the stairs to get one.

Tony Vavlas

Me: OK, so we'll put one in your upstairs freezer for when you need it.

Dad: There's no room. Why don't you take them home and when I need one I can just call you?

Me: Dad, I really don't have the room either. Why don't we just throw these out and if you need an ice pack I'll make you one?

Dad: I also thought they'd be great to throw in a cooler to keep pop and beer cold.

Me: Do you have a cooler?

Dad: No. Do you?

Me: Yes.

Dad: See, you need these more than me. I knew I kept them for a reason. You're welcome.

Me: But… I really don't… Thanks Dad.

I now have an Igloo cooler filled with medical ice packs which were once used to soothe various sore body parts. If anybody wants to borrow six or seven of them, just let me know.

☎
work phone

In my line of work, my phone rings nonstop between 8 am and 6 pm. I am based out of an office in my home and when my Dad finds out I'm working from home he loses the concept that it's still work, even if I'm home. He'll call for the most bizarre reasons, and before you all say "He's lonely!" forget that! He spends his days out and about with friends and family, and I either visit or talk to him EVERY day.

Some recent phone calls… Each one a different ring of my WORK phone.

—What is Alfalfa's [from the Little Rascals] real name?

—Was Alfalfa in any other movies?

—Turn on Turner Classic Movies. Is that Alfalfa?

—Can I make a peanut butter and jelly sandwich with raspberry jelly or does it have to be grape or strawberry?

—Klondike Bars come in Caramel Pretzel flavor now.

—Have you tried the Caramel Pretzel Klondike Bars yet?

—Come over and get one of these Klondike Bars!!!

—What kind of doctor is Dr. Phil? Medical or scientifical?

—How can you tell if a squirrel is sick?

—My squirrel in my tree seems "mopey!" Look out your window and see what you think. [Maybe he should call Dr. Phil.]

—Happy Groundhog's Day. [On JANUARY 2nd]

—Can I wear a Browns jacket to a funeral? [What better place to wear a Browns jacket?]

—Are you working from home today?

—Did I call your work phone? I meant to call your home phone. [Doesn't make a difference, they're both on my desk.]

—What time are you taking a lunch break? Can we go to New Castle for chili dogs? [It's a two hour trip.]

—Working from home again? Want to go to the mall with me to pick out a pair of dress shoes?

—There's definitely something wrong with that squirrel! He seems depressed! [It's eight degrees out!!! Who wouldn't be?]

—You sound annoyed… are you? If you had a secretary, she could answer all of my questions and I wouldn't have to bother YOU!

Tony Vavlas

gps

Rrriiinnnggg

Me: Hello.

Dad: I'm getting new glasses. Do you think I should get the scratch resistant coating on the lenses?

Me: Yes, DEFINITELY!!! And you should get an amber colored pair for night driving. While you're at it, you've broken or lost seven pairs of glasses last year, ask them about a carbon fiber titanium protective case and GPS tracking too.

Six days later...

Rrriiinnnggg

(Lens Express on caller ID)

Me: Hello.

L.E.: Hello Tony?

Me: Yes.

L.E.: Hi Tony. We've got your father, Anthony, here and he's getting glasses. He said that you told him about a few options that he should get but he couldn't remember what they were.

Me: I told him to get the scratch resistant lenses and the amber coating on one pair for night driving. It would also be helpful if they had GPS for tracking them down, and came in a protective case that could withstand a nuclear explosion.

L.E.: We don't have some of those options.

Me: Oh. That is most unfortunate. Take a good look at his face then. You are going to be seeing him... A LOT!!!

australia

I spent the day with my Dad today. Within five minutes in my car, he had lost both his eyeglasses and sunglasses under the seat. While trying on shoes he lost his eyedrops and a calculator fell out of his pocket.

Me: Dad, why do you carry a calculator around? You know you have a calculator on your phone… right?

Dad: Yeah, I know that, but the last time I tried to use it was at the bowling alley, totalling scores. I accidentally called Australia.

shakira, part 1

Rrriiinnnggg

Dad: Hey, I need your help putting something up in the rafters of my garage.

Me: OK, be right over.

Dad: Hurry!!!

(Arriving moments later)

Me: What's up?

Dad: I need you to hang my Shakira poster up in my garage.

Me: Really Dad? That's a LITTLE creepy!

Dad: Just do it or I'm getting on the ladder myself!

Me: OK!

Dad: You know I'm going to marry her someday!

Me: Well I'd make your move fast! Your window of compatibility is

Tony Vavlas

slamming shut as we speak!

Dad: No! She likes older men.

Me: Well, you've got THAT going for you.

Dad: Wouldn't you like Shakira as your stepmom?

Me: Sure, I'd be the envy of fifth period lunch. I can hardly wait to tell my friends.

Dad: Smartass!!! I'm cutting you out of my will.

Me: Well maybe "mommy" will add me to hers!

Dad: And just why would she do that?

Me: In exchange for helping her get a restraining order against YOU!!!

Dad: Shut up!!! That poster is crooked!

Me: Not as crooked as your dirty little mind!

☎
extra value meal

One summer day…

Rrriiinnnggg

Me: Hello Dad.

Dad: Hey! Do you want a bag of Big Macs?

Me: You ask that like you have an EXTRA bag of Big Macs.

Dad: I do. And an extra bag of fries and a tray of drinks too.

Me: And just how does one obtain an EXTRA bag of Big Macs and fries?

Dad: Well… the van ahead of me at the drive through pulled

away after ordering. I pulled up to the first window and paid with my card without paying attention to the total. Then I pulled to the second window and they handed me two bags, then another two, and then two trays of drinks. I wasn't paying attention. I just figured they gave me a special combo meal deal.

Me: What did you order?

Dad: Two cheeseburgers and two small fries off of the dollar menu for me and Joe.

Me: And you didn't figure it out when they handed you four bags and two trays of drinks?

Dad: I wasn't paying attention. I was hungry and just wanted my food.

Me: A second bag would have been "not paying attention" but when they handed you a third and fourth bag… well, that's just being oblivious.

Dad: I told you, I was HUNGRY. You know I can't think when I smell food!!! Especially McDonald's french fries!!!

Me: So how much did lunch off of the value menu cost you this time?

Dad: $36 and change. I didn't realize they charged me so much until I came home. Come on over and get a bag or two. Me and Joe are stuffed.

Me: I'm about to go walk at the park.

Dad: Well take some of these and pass them out up there.

Me: I'm NOT gonna do that Dad. I'll get arrested. I'll talk to you later.

Dad: Take one and eat while you walk.

Me: No thanks. I'll talk to you later.

Dad: Why do you have to be so unreasonable?

Tony Vavlas

lost

Rrriiinnnggg

Me: Hello.

Dad: Hey… I need you to come over and help me find something.

Me: I'm working right now. Just take out your St. Anthony statue and say a prayer. That usually works.

Dad: I know, but that is what's lost. I couldn't find my car keys so I went to get my St. Anthony statue to say a prayer and I can't find it.

Me: You lost the statue of the saint that you pray to when you want to find lost stuff?

Dad: Yep.

Me: You better pray to your St. Jude statue. He is the patron Saint of Lost Causes.

gift

Rrriiinnnggg

Me: Hello.

Dad: Can you help me get some of my mail together to be mailed Monday?

Me: Sure.

Dad: You address the envelopes and stuff them and I'll put on the return address stickers.

Me: OK.

(I address twelve envelopes and stuff them accordingly as Dad puts on the stickers).

Me: Dad, are you a little late sending out your Christmas cards?

Dad: No. Why?

Me: Because you just used twelve gift tags instead of return address labels.

Dad: OK… you write from Tony Vavlas and my address on all of them.

Me: Just put a return address label over those stickers. You have a million of them.

Dad: Well THAT will look stupid!

Me: And keeping the gift tags on with your name filled in won't?

Dad: No! It looks kinda classy! Like I'm sending them a gift.

Me: I'm sure the folks at Armstrong Cable, Erie Insurance, and MedCo are gonna be soooooo impressed!

not getting out

Rrriiinnnggg

Dad: Hello.

Me: Hey Dad, wanna run to the store with me? I need a few things at Giant Eagle.

Dad: No.

Me: C'mon. It'll do you some good to get out.

Dad: OK. But I'm not getting out of the car.

Me: OK.

Thirty minutes later…

Dad: *(As I load HIS four Giant Eagle bags into my trunk)* OK… now we need to stop at Marc's and Walmart.

Me: What happened to "no I don't want to go and I'm not getting out of the car?"

Dad: Shut up and drive.

outside the box

Rrriiinnnggg

Me: Hello.

Dad: Have you seen the new *Sports Illustrated* Swimsuit Edition? One of the guys had it down at the bowling alley.

Me: No Dad... I haven't seen it.

Dad: There is one girl in there wearing nothing but body paint.

Me: Oh yeah? You like that, huh???

Dad: Yeah... I'd really like to see her in a tight sweater.

Me: Way to think outside the box Dad!!!

e-mailman

Rrriiinnnggg

Me: Hello.

Dad: Marie sent me some pictures to my e-mail. Can you help me open my e-mail?

Me: Sure. Did you give her your e-mail address?

Dad: Yeah... 437 Whipple Ave dot com. Right?

Me: Yep... that's it. Now we just have to sit and wait for the e-mailman to deliver it.

Dad: Oh... so maybe Monday?

☎
geeked up

Dad: What are you doing?

Me: Throwing eggshells out in the yard for the animals.

Dad: Why?

Me: Because it gives them calcium. Animals need calcium for strong teeth and bones.

Dad: I've never seen a squirrel on crutches in our neighborhood.

Me: See! It's working.

Dad: I don't think they eat them.

Me: Well, they're always gone.

Dad: That's because I run them over with the riding lawnmower?

Me: The eggshells or the animals?

Dad: A little of both. Hey! Do those eggshells work on all wild animals?

Me: Yes. Why?

Dad: Because the last thing I need is some wolf or bigfoot wandering through my yard all geeked up on eggshells. I wouldn't stand a chance. I want them as weak as possible.

Me: Just throw your tractor into high gear!!!

☎

the vinny challenge

Rrriiinnnggg

Dad: Hello.

Me: Hey Dad. I need a favor, I need you to dump a bucket of ice water on my head.

Dad: Sure… but that's just stupid. Dr. Oz said that some people are dying of heart attacks after they do that.

Me: I'm not gonna die of a heart attack. Some people also die after eating at questionable Chinese buffets… but that hasn't stopped you.

Dad: True. I don't understand how dumping a bucket of ice water on your head can cure a disease. In fact… you might even get a cold from it.

Me: It doesn't cure the disease. It just brings awareness to it.

Dad: Well that doesn't make any sense at all. You already are aware of it.

Me: But I have to film it, challenge some other folks, and then post the video to the internet to raise awareness for ALS. And then I also donate $10.

Dad: You have to pay to get a bucket of water dumped on your head? Who's runnin' this racket? The mob?

Me: No Dad, if I don't accept the challenge I have to donate $100 to ALS.

Dad: Well that definitely sounds like it's mob run to me. That's the way they operate.

Me: Just put on a Browns shirt and meet me in your driveway in 10 minutes.

Dad: OK… but if a guy named Vinny calls me after this, I ain't answering!!!

☎
emergency

Rrriiinnnggg

Me: Hello?

Dad: Come over here quick! I need your help! It's an emergency!!!

((((I run to Dad's house.))))

Me: *((((Out of breath)))* What's wrong?!?

Dad: I lost my reading glasses and my driving glasses.

Me: Let me help you out with the definition of EMERGENCY!!!

Dad: I was cutting the grass and I think I dropped my reading glasses in the yard while cutting.

Me: Were you taking in a novel while you were on the tractor?

Dad: No but I had to put gas in the tractor and I needed the glasses to see the gas.

Me: You have two containers in the garage: GAS and BLUE windshield washer fluid. Do you need me to mark them with braille? What about your driving [amber] glasses? They should be in the car right? There's no reason to take DRIVING glasses out of your CAR.

Dad: I stopped at a friend's house last night and I may have left them at his house.

Me: Is there a big problem with headlight glare on his couch?

Dad: No... not really! Shut up and help me find my glasses!!!

Me: I'm looking!

Dad: Maybe I should get contacts.

Me: Or a nurse!

Tony Vavlas

uncracked

Rrriiinnnggg

Me: Hey Dad, what's up?

Dad: Are you going to the store today?

Me: Sure, I'll go. What do you need.

Dad: I need six dozen of eggs from Aldi's and a quart and a half of milk.

Me: A quart and a half huh? That's pretty obscure. How about a gallon?

Dad: That's too much! OK get me a half gallon.

Me: You sure you only want a half gallon? I'll get you a gallon.

Dad: That's too much!

Me: This is the third time in a week that you've had me buy milk for you. I think you're safe with a gallon!

Dad: I'll never use all that milk.

Me: A gallon of milk is too much but you want six dozen eggs???

Dad: The eggs are for a friend.

Me: Well share the gallon of milk with her too.

Dad: Make sure that you check the eggs for cracks.

Me: OK… do you want cracked or uncracked ones?

Dad: Uncracked please!

<<<**CLICK.**>>>

☎

a peck

Today at Apple Castle Orchard in New Castle, Pennsylvania.

Dad: Do you have honeycrisp apples?

Apple Castle Employee: We sure do. Would you like a peck?

Dad: No thank you honey! Just the apples. I don't kiss on the first date.

☎

the first stop on the way to heaven

One late summer day, Dad and I were treated to an Indians double header in a fancy corporate suite by Ken and David Kish.

As we walked down the very exclusive corridor towards our suite...

Dad: Hey Ton.

Me: Yeah Dad?

Dad: Start looking for Mom.

Me: Huh?

Dad: I think we might be in Heaven.

Doorman: Enjoy the game gentlemen.

Dad: Thank you St. Peter.

Me: I think Heaven would have more familiar faces.

Dad: Maybe this is just the first stop on the way to Heaven. If they put us on a bus next that says Browns Super Bowl party... start listening for harp music.

Tony Vavlas

☎
thirty-something

Rrriiinnnggg

Me: Hello.

Dad: Hey! The moon is only going to be thirty miles from the earth tonight and shooting stars are going to be coming out of it. You going to watch?

Me: Probably not.

Dad: But you like those kinds of things. I figured you'd watch it.

Me: I'll be too busy buying a boat.

Dad: A boat?

Me: Yeah, if the moon is going to be that close to the earth, it would mess up the tides and cause massive flooding. We're gonna need a boat. And lots of supplies. I'll save you a seat. Are you sure that's what you heard?

Dad: Yep… right on the six o'clock news.

Me: Are you sure you didn't hear that there will be a super moon tonight which will be thirty percent brighter than a normal full moon. And that there is supposed to be the annual Perseid meteor shower going on tonight as well?

Dad: Yeah… maybe that's what they said.

Me: Missed the mark on that one Dad.

Dad: I got the thirty right!

sewage

Rrriiinnnggg

Me: Hello.

Dad: Hey, I need you to pick me up some sewage to feed the birds.

Me: You mean suet?

Dad: Probably.

paula

Rrriiinnnggg

Me: Hello.

Dad: What ever happened to Paula Abdul Jabbar?

Me: She's a converted Catholic who goes by the name Louise Alcindor now.

uptnwn phxza

Rrriiinnnggg

Dad: How do I text on my phone?

Me: You don't!

Dad: I want to learn how.

Me: It costs like $3 per text extra.

Dad: You told me we had UNLIMITED texting!

Me: CRAP! Oh sure, you remember *that!* Your phone doesn't have a keyboard. It makes texting difficult.

Dad: Do I do it the same way that I type names into my address book?

Me: Yes, but your address book is filled with entries like Uptnwn Phxza and Dnbtor Franhnpolos.

Tony Vavlas

Dad: I can do it! Just show me where I go on my phone to text.

Two days later...

Gling TEXT FROM DAD

Nneed a ha;d gblloon of mikj. And not any od that B% crap eitheq!!!

a familiar number

Rrriiinnnggg

Dad: Hello.

Me: Hey Dad... do you have Joe's cell phone number? I want to ask him if I could borrow his rototiller to dig the garden.

Dad: Yeah, I have it but good luck, he never answers his cell phone. Wait, here it is 330-398-47XX.

(I dial the number, which seems strangely familiar.)

Rrriiinnnggg

Dad: Hello.

Me: Dad, that's YOUR cell phone number that you gave me.

Dad: Oh I have it in my phone under JOE. No wonder he never answers when I call!!!

Me: Oh Boy!!!

☎

steve

Rrriiinnnggg

Me: Hello.

Dad: Are you watching ESPN? Steve Greenberg is talking about the Browns.

Me: Who the heck is Steve Greenberg?

Dad: The skinny guy on *Mike & Mike.*

Me: The host? You mean Mike Greenberg?

Dad: Yeah… the host… the skinny Jewish guy. I'm pretty sure his name is Steve.

Me: So he's the host of a show called *Mike & Mike* and you think his name is Steve.

Dad: Maybe it is Mike… and never mind. It was the Bengals. I just saw the orange helmets.

the fair

Rrriiinnnggg

Dad: Hello.

Me: Hey Dad, are you going to the Canfield Fair this year?

Dad: Why should I pay good money to stand elbow to elbow with some deodorant challenged hillbillies while overpaying for a sausage sandwich which will probably give me food poisoning, that I'll have to eat standing over a trash can while bees swarm my head? Oh I know, because I'll get to do it all accompanied by the smell of cow shit and if I'm lucky I just might step in some and bring some of that fair goodness home with me. I'll drive thirteen miles to park fifteen miles away and wait for a tractor to pick me up to take me to see things that I have absolutely no interest in seeing anyway!!!

Me: Geez Dad… breathe!!! I just asked you if you were gonna go this year.

Dad: Yeah… I'll probably go.

Tony Vavlas

☎

new wave

Rrriiinnnggg

Dad: I ordered a NuWave oven and it was buy one get one so I'm giving one to you.

Me: Thanks Dad!! I can finally try out those Depeche Mode meatloaf and Echo & the Bunnymen muffin recipes that I've been holding on to since the 80s.

Dad: You're welcome but I don't understand.

Me: It would scare me if you did Dad!

☎

smoke detector

Rrriiinnnggg

Me: Hello?

Dad: What are you doing?

Me: I'm about to eat dinner. What's up?

Dad: Do you have a 9 volt battery?

Me: Yes. I'll run it over right after dinner.

Dad: I need it now. My smoke detector battery is dead.

Me: OK. Can it wait until after dinner?

Dad: No. Didn't you hear me? My smoke detector is dead!!

Me: You're awake, aren't you?

Dad: Yes.

Me: And your nose is in working order, right?

Dad: Yes.

Me: Then your smoke detector isn't dead.

Dad: But I need that battery now.

Me: Are you planning a fireworks show in your house in the next half hour?

Dad: No.

Me: Are you planning on rubbing two sticks together rapidly, smoking near a powder keg, or shuffling your feet together on a nylon carpet while carrying a jar of grain alcohol in the next thirty minutes?

Dad: I don't think so.

Me: Then it could probably wait!!!

Dad: But the guy on television said that you should check your smoke detectors periodically and change the batteries if necessary.

Me: But that guy had probably already eaten dinner!!!

Dad: If you'd stop arguing with me you could have already brought me the battery.

<<<*CLICK.*>>>

~ ~ ~ ~ ~ *(I take the battery to Dad's.)* ~ ~ ~ ~ ~

Me: Here you go Dad, one 9 volt battery.

Dad: OK. Just put it on the counter. I'll change it after the Ohio State game.

slim jims

Rrriiinnnggg

Me: Hello.

Tony Vavlas

Dad: Hey, come over and get these Slim Jims that Joe [the neighbor] gave to me to give to you.

The next morning...

Rrriiinnnggg

Me: Hello.

Dad: Hey, did you eat any of those Slim Jims?

Me: Yeah.

Dad: How were they?

Me: They were OK. Not great... but edible.

Dad: Oh... well they were dog treats that his dog wouldn't eat. He gave them to me to give to you to give to your DOG. How do you feel?

Me: All of a sudden I have the urge to chase cars and bite you.

☎

acceptable loses

Rrriiinnnggg

Dad: Hello.

Me: Hey Dad! Where were you all day yesterday?

Dad: I went down to the track on a bus trip, to play slots.

Me: How'd you do?

Dad: I lost.

Me: How bad?

Dad: Just a pair of sunglasses and my garage door opener. I may have dropped them on the bus?

Me: Not too bad. You're getting better!!!

Dad: I know! I still had my car and house keys when they dropped me off this time.

space something

Dad: I need you to make me a tape.

Me: You mean a CD Dad?

Dad: Whatever!

Me: What kind of CD?

Dad: You know... That guy with the hats... Space something.

Me: Bruno Mars?

Dad: That's it!!!

Me: I'm not sure what scares me more. That I understood you or that you want a Bruno Mars CD!

expert

Rrriiinnnggg

Me: Hello.

Dad: Hey, Cousin Bob called and he wants MY recipes for chili and pasta fagioli. I promised I'd give them to him.

Me: OK. Do you need me to type them up for you?

Dad: Yes! And one other thing...

Me: Sure, what's up?

Dad: Can you give him YOUR recipes because I've never made chili or pasta fagioli!

Tony Vavlas

Me: So you promised him recipes for stuff you've never made? Good thing he called an expert!!

☎
charlie's web

Rrriiinnnggg

Me: Hello.

Dad: Hey! There's a HUGE spider on the inside of my garage door and every time I open it I'm afraid he's going to jump on my head!

Me: I'm working now Dad. Can't you just kill it?

Dad: NO! You shouldn't kill spiders outside. They eat other bugs.

Me: Bugs that are creepier than spiders?

Dad: Probably not, but hurry! Catch him and get him outta my garage!

~ ~ ~ ~ ~ *(Walk to Dad's house.)* ~ ~ ~ ~ ~

(((Swat!!!)))<<<SQUISH!!!>>>Problem solved!

~ ~ ~ ~ ~ *(Walk back home.)* ~ ~ ~ ~ ~

Rrriiinnnggg

Me: Hello.

Dad: Did you get him?

Me: Yes!

Dad: You killed him didn't you?

Me: Nooooooooo! I have him saved in a jar. Later on I'm gonna take him for a ride out in the country and give him to a farmer who has been looking for a huge venomous spider for his farm, to help control the other bugs.

Dad: Oh! Good Job! Tell the farmer that his name is Charlie and he really likes to eat crickets.

☎

ponarangles

Rrriiinnnggg

Me: Hello.

Dad: Hey! I bought you some ponarangles.

Me: Pomegranates?

Dad: Whatever!

Me: Thanks Dad!

☎

starbucks

Rrriiinnnggg

Me: Hello.

Dad: Hey... I ordered a coffee at Starbucks and my total was over $4. Did I do something wrong?

Me: You mean besides going to Starbucks?

☎

tool belt

Rrriiinnnggg

Dad: Hey! Come over quick. I was getting a shower and the shower handle came off and I can't shut off the water.

~ ~ ~ ~ (Walk to Dad's house.) ~ ~ ~ ~

<<<Knock Knock Knock>>>

!!!!! Dad answers the door NAKED!!!!!

Tony Vavlas

Me: Dad!!! What the HELL? Where are your clothes?

Dad: I told you, I was in the shower.

Me: WAS in the shower. Past tense. Put some clothes on!

Dad: I thought I might have to help you fix it and I didn't want to get my clothes wet.

Me: So you thought it would be OK to get into the shower WITH me to fix it… while not wearing clothes???

Dad: We're family!

Me: Oh!! Right!!! Then by all means, let me take off my clothes too!

Dad: THAT would be weird!!!

Me: And THIS isn't? This is like a bad episode of *National Geographic* meets *This Old House*.

Dad: OK!! But I don't want to get my clothes wet!

Me: Could you at least put on a tool belt? PLEASE!!!

☎
the time guy

Rrriiinnnggg

Dad: Hey! What in the hell time is it? I changed some of my clocks last night but not all of them and now I'm confused.

Me: It's 5:32 am Dad. Is something wrong?

Dad: Yes, I told you… all of my clocks are on different times!

Me: Dad!!! It's 5:32 AM. On my day OFF. This call couldn't have waited until a REASONABLE time?

Dad: I tried calling 330-747-1411 but the guy's not there anymore. Do you have his new number?

Me: What guy?

Dad: The time and temp guy at 330-747-1411.

Me: How far back did you turn your clock? That number hasn't been up and running in twenty years. That guy's long gone!

Dad: That's a shame that they let him go!

Me: I know! First Ye Olde Towne Crier. Now THIS!!!

Dad: Who?

Me: Never mind. Just check your cell phone!

Dad: The guy's new number is on my cell phone?

Me: NO!!! But your cell phone will always give you the correct time!

Dad: Oh!!!! Well why didn't you just tell me that?

Me: I did, when we turned the clocks back last year, and you called me at 5:30 am.

☎

moon

(Dad mooning a passing car.)

Me: Dad!!! What do you think you're doing???

Dad: That's just Judie… the City Administrator. She's always picking on me when I see her so I moon her Mini Cooper every time she goes by.

Me: That's real cute Dad… except that that wasn't a Mini Cooper and it wasn't Judie!

☎

wet deer

Every autumn since I was sixteen, my Dad has given me the same two pieces of driving advice. It's deer mating season, you gotta watch out for deer. And, Be careful, wet leaves are as slippery as ice.

The other day I was driving him to the store...

Me: Hey Dad! Aren't you going to give me my annual autumn driving lesson?

Dad: Oh yeah. It's deer mating season, you gotta be careful. Wet deer are as slippery as ice.

Me: Haha! I don't want to know how you know that!

Dad: Shut up and watch the road!

☎
greek, american, or bulgarian?

Eating lunch at a small local diner recently... with Dad!

Waitress: Are you ready to order?

Dad: Is the feta in your Greek salad Greek feta or domesticated?

Waitress: I'll find out.

(She leaves.)

Me: DOMESTIC Dad! Not domesticated. Domestic feta is made here in the U.S. Domesticated is the opposite of wild. It means tamed. Like the opposite of a wild cat is a domesticated cat.

Dad: Well, there could be domesticated feta... made from domesticated sheep and cows.

(The waitress returns.)

Waitress: Feta is a Greek cheese sir. The cook says so.

Dad: Oh I know honey! But is the feta made here or in Greece?

Waitress: I'll find out.

(She leaves again.)

Me: So you really think that some feta is made from the milk of wild cows and wild sheep? Who is milking these wild animals?

Dad: Very skilled milkers, I suppose.

Me: They'd have to be pretty darned skilled Dad!

Dad: That's why it's so expensive. They have to sneak up on the animals.

(The waitress returns again.)

Waitress: The cook says we don't make it here. We buy it from a supplier.

Dad: Ask the cook if it's imported from Greece or if it's American feta.

(The waitress leaves again.)

Me: The salad is $3.99 Dad! At that price it shouldn't require that the poor girl does a research paper in order to serve it to you. And at $3.99, I think we can safely assume that no highly skilled wild ninja stealth milkers were involved.

(The waitress returns again.)

Waitress: It's American.

Dad: I'll take it!

Me: American feta is better than Greek?

Dad: No. They both taste like crap compared to Bulgarian feta but at $3.99 who's gonna pass that up?

Me: I'll take a reuben and a side of french fries.

Dad: Are the french fries from domesticated or French potatoes?

Waitress: I'll find out.

Tony Vavlas

(The waitress leaves again.)

Me: You are evil. You're gonna tip her like she served you Bulgarian feta on a gold platter and fed you by hand!!! This is why lunch with you takes three hours!!!

☎

the price of sanity

Ever wonder what the price of sanity is? I can tell you. It's 47 cents.

Rrriiinnnggg

Me: Hello.

Dad: Can you pick me up a gift bag at the Dollar Store?

Me: Sure.

Dad: Don't pay more than $1.50.

(I drop off the bag to Dad.)

Dad: How much do I owe you?

Me: Don't worry about it Dad!

Dad: How much was it??

Me: Really Dad. It's OK.

Dad: Tell me!!

Me: $1.97

Dad: $1.97?!? Are you out of your damned mind?

(Dad hands me $5)

Dad: Keep the change. The rest is for gas.

☎
the clicker

Rrriiinnnggg

Me: Hello Dad!

<Click>

Rrriiinnnggg

Me: Hello Dad!!!

<Click>

Rrriiinnnggg

Me: HELLO DAD!!!

<Click>

///I DIAL DAD's NUMBER///

Me: Dad… Why do you keep calling me and hanging up? Is everything OK?

Dad: I was just trying to open a picture that you sent me. Don't I have to go to your number to open it?

Me: No Dad. You can go to the message I sent you with the picture or to your saved pictures. Do you need me to come over to help??

Dad: No. I got this.

Me: OK.

Rrriiinnnggg

Me: Hello Dad!

<Click>

30 minutes or less

The trash pick up in our town has been delayed this week due to a union strike. I had this brief conversation with Dad today before he hung up on me.

Rrriiinnnggg

Me: Hello.

Dad: Why wasn't there trash DELIVERY today?

Me: They changed the way they do it. They don't just bring you random stuff anymore. You have to place an order. Thirty minutes or less or it's free.

<<<*CLICK.*>>>

heater

Rrriiinnnggg

Me: Hello Dad!

Dad: *(In a boastful tone)* Come on over and see my new Eden Pure Electric Heater.

Me: OK. Be right over.

~ ~ ~ ~ *(Walk to Dad's.)* ~ ~ ~ ~

Me: How much did that set you back?

Dad: About $200

Me: I think a $15 ceramic heater may have done the same thing for you.

Dad: This one is endorsed by Bob Vila.

Me: Bob Vila is the Dr. Oz of home improvement… a QUACK!!!

Dad: Zip your lip and help me get this out of the box.

//unbox// //setup// //plug in// //turn on//

(Poof!!! DARKNESS!!)

Me: You blew a breaker.

(Down the stairs we go to reset the breaker.)

Dad: Let me try another outlet.

(Poof!!! More DARKNESS!!)

(Down the stairs we go to reset the breaker AGAIN!!!)

Dad: Something's wrong!!

Me: Oh… You think? You mean that's not supposed to happen?

Dad: Shut up! Let's try this outlet behind the couch.

//move couch// //plug in//

(POOF!!! DARKNESS returns.)

(Downstairs for a third time to reset the breaker.)

Me: Dad, I think you got taken.

Dad: What do you mean? This thing works great.

Me: Uhhhh… No it doesn't!

Dad: Yes it does. After three trips up and down the stairs and moving the couch, I'm so warm I'm sweating.

☎
clearing the calendar

Rrriiinnnggg

Me: Hello.

Tony Vavlas

Dad: Hey… come over. I bought you some mocha cappuccino cookies. They are really good.

Me: OK… I'll be over a little bit later.

~ ~ ~ ~ (Walk to Dad's a few hours later.) ~ ~ ~ ~ ~

Me: Dad… there are only three cookies left.

Dad: I know… I told you they are good. I ate them.

Me: Well, do you have any plans tomorrow?

Dad: Yeah… I have a lot to do tomorrow.

Me: Well, you better cancel. Those are sugar free cookies and it says on the package that eating more than two might have a slight laxative effect. How many did you eat.

Dad: About fifteen. That can't happen… I gotta run errands tomorrow.

Me: Maybe RUN was a poor choice of words Dad.

☎
minty fresh

Rrriiinnnggg

Me: Hello Dad.

Dad: Hey! Get over here quick! I spilled a bottle of tonic water and it spilled all under the fridge. I need help.

Me: Be right there!

~ ~ ~ ~ (Walk to Dad's.) ~ ~ ~ ~

Me: I need a bucket with hot water and Mr. Clean in it and I'll move the fridge.

Dad: OK.

(Gets bucket)

Me: Dad, what kind of Mr. Clean is this? It smells like mint!

Dad: Aw CRAP!!! It's SCOPE.

Me: That's OK. It won't hurt the floor. I'll just get new water and re-do it. Where's the Mr. Clean?

Dad: Probably under the bathroom sink. I think I've been gargling with it!

☎

cold case

Rrriiinnnggg

Me: Hello Dad!

Dad: I think my freezer is broken.

Me: Why's that?

Dad: My ice cube trays are all empty. Did you come over and take all of my ice?

Me: Nope Dad! Wasn't me! Is everything else frozen in your freezer?

Dad: Yes.

Me: Well then it appears that the freezer is working fine. Why do you think it's broken?

Dad: Because my ice cube trays are empty AND all of the stuff in my freezer is stuck together and covered in ice. I'm telling you, this freezer is broken.

Me: Hmmmmmm… I just don't know, detective. Let me know if you break the case! Did you happen to fill the trays shortly before dropping the bottle of tonic water the other day?

Dad: Yes.

Tony Vavlas

Me: And I moved your refrigerator.

Dad: Yes.

Me: Well THAT's when the "break" occurred.

Dad: I knew it!!! YOU broke my freezer!!!

☎
early bird

(9:15 am, Thanksgiving Morning)

Rrriiinnnggg

Me: Hello?

Dad: What temperature does a turkey have to be for it to be done?

Me: At least 165 degrees. About 4½ hours at 325 degrees in the oven.

Dad: Oh good. It's done!

Me: At 9:15 am? The parade has barely even started. What time did you get up?

Dad: About 4:30.

Me: What did you stuff it with? Waffles??? You'll be eating leftovers before most of us have finished round one.

Dad: I'm thankful YOU'RE not cooking for me! We wouldn't be eating until noon.

☎
the game

I live next door to my Dad and I often look out the window to make sure everything is OK at his house. A few nights ago...

Rrriiinnnggg

Me: Hey Dad, why is it dark at your house so early but I keep seeing flashes of light in the window?

Dad: Oh! Because Angel [the cat] has static electricity and if I cover her with a blanket and pull it off really fast, sparks shoot off of her. It's a game we play.

Me: You're doing WHAT??? Oh Man!!! Am I ever sorry I asked!!! Are you at least winning?

flea market

Rrriiinnnggg

Me: Hello.

Dad: Guess what they were throwing away at the flea market!!!

Me: Dad, In the history of history, I can guarantee you that nothing GOOD has ever followed the phrase, "Guess what they were throwing away at the flea market!" I don't think I want to know.

pot

Dad: Look at that… a marijuana leaf on that van. In my day, people were ashamed of their vices. They got theirs displayed.

Me: Dad! That's an OSU sticker. It's a Buckeye leaf.

Dad: Oh! Well by the way they're playing lately they'd get more respect with the pot sticker.

rainforest

Me: My God Dad!!! Why is it so hot in here?

Dad: I turned the furnace up because I was cold, then fell asleep and forgot about it .

Tony Vavlas

Me: The walls are all sweating and your cabinet doors won't open. You have a state of the art furnace with an electronically controlled humidifier. I think you can lose the bowls of water in front of every register.

Dad: If it gets too dry in here I get dry skin.

Me: I think you're safe. It's like a rainforest in here. The little guy on your weather station that tells you if it's going to rain or be clear is wearing a grass skirt and has a bone through his nose.

droppings

Rrriiinnnggg

Me: Hello Dad.

Dad: Hey!!! I forgot to buy turkey gravy. Can I make gravy out of the droppings?

Me: Haha… Yeah but it'll taste like crap!!! You mean DRIPPINGS!!!

Dad: No, I'm pretty sure I mean droppings.

Me: You want to make gravy out of turkey droppings?

Dad: YES!!!

Me: Hahahahaha!!!

Dad: Never mind. I'll use chicken gravy.

mr. leggs

Rrriiinnnggg

Me: What do you want for Christmas Dad?

Dad: You know what… I could really use some new jeans. Mr. Leggs brand.

Me: Mr. Leggs??? I don't even think they make those anymore.

Dad: Yes they do. I just bought a pair.

Me: Where'd you find them?

Dad: Bargain Port.

Me: Dad!!! Bargain Port has been closed for more than twenty years. And it was a hardware store.

Dad: Well go on the internet and see who sells them now.

Me: When you bought your last pair were they called jeans or dungarees??

Dad: Very funny. Don't be buying me any of those new Brett Favre jeans with the U-shaped crotch

Me: What shape crotch did Mr. Leggs have?

Dad: I don't know but they fit. Probably W.

Me: OK, so really… What do you want??

Dad: I told you. Mr. Leggs jeans.

Me: Jeans that don't exist from a hardware store that doesn't exist??? Gift card it is!!!

greens

Rrriiinnnggg

Me: Hello Dad.

Dad: Hey, I went to Bogey's Restaurant and got some greens. I have some left. You can have them for dinner tonight.

Me: I'm making coconut shrimp. I'm not sure if that goes too well with greens.

Tony Vavlas

Dad: You can eat these with the shrimp. It'll be good.

Me: How about if you just keep them and have them for lunch tomorrow.

Dad: No, just come and get them. I can't possibly eat any more greens. You can have them for dinner.

Me: I don't know Dad, maybe later.

Dad: Don't cook anything else. Just shut up and come get these now.

$$\sim \; \sim \; \sim \; \sim \textbf{\textit{(Walk to Dad's.)}} \sim \; \sim \; \sim \; \sim$$

Me: Dad… REALLY!!! This is what you were making such a big deal about? It's like a tablespoon of greens. In fact you probably shouldn't even refer to it as greens. It's more like a green.

Dad: I didn't want them to go to waste.

Me: You've got more greens stuck in your teeth right now than there are in the container.

Dad: Well add to it.

Me: Add what??

Dad: Some more greens.

Me: Dad, I didn't want greens in the first place. I only came over because you are insistent. Now you have me making a batch of greens and adding this tablespoon of leftover greens to it.

Dad: If you make greens, bring me some over.

Me: I thought you said you couldn't possibly eat any more greens.

Dad: But I like YOUR greens.

Me: Well apparently you liked these too. There's only a tablespoon left.

Dad: Why can't you just appreciate something when somebody gives it to you?

Me: You're right Dad. I'm sorry. Thanks for the greens.

Dad: You're welcome. What time will YOUR greens be done?

cool and no-so-cool docs

Shopping with Dad… I stop for new work shoes.

Dad: What kind of shoes are those?

Me: Doc Martens. I love them. They are really comfortable.

Dad: I have those.

Me: No Dad, you have Dr. Scholl's.

Dad: What's the difference?

Me: About $70 and hundred "cool points."

legit

Rrriiinnnggg

Me: Hello Dad!

Dad: Come over and read this. I think I won a contest.

Me: I didn't know they had a goofiest Dad contest.

Dad: Shut up and get over here and read this. I'm a winner.

Me: OK. But just like the last time… you didn't win a contest.

Dad: How do you know?

Me: Did you enter any contests?

Dad: No.

Me: Then what makes you think you could win any contests.

Tony Vavlas

Dad: Just get over here and read this for me.

~ ~ ~ ~ ~ (Walk to Dad's.) ~ ~ ~ ~ ~

Dad: Look! All good prizes. A car, $10,000, a boat, or $500 in gift cards.

Me: Let me see.

(I read the sweepstakes offer.)

Me: Dad… here's the hook. It's not $500 in gift cards. It's $500 in gift COUPONS.

Dad: What's the difference?

Me: Gift cards are gift cards. Gift coupons are coupons. They total $500 off. Probably a hundred coupons with $5 off each.

Dad: Well that's a ripoff!

Me: That's why I tell you to just throw those things away.

Dad: Well maybe I won one of the other prizes.

Me: You didn't. You never entered a contest. Why would they just proclaim you the winner of a contest you never entered?

Dad: So why do they send me these things.

Me: Same reason the gas company and phone company send you mail. They want money.

Dad: How do they get my name?

Me: Every casino you go to makes you sign up for a "membership" card right? They sell your name to these sweepstakes. Then they send you mail because they already know you like to gamble. Just like a slot machine, the sweepstakes will lead you along making you believe you are close to winning. Next thing you know you've sent them a lot of cash and won nothing.

Dad: That's kinda scary.

Me: Yeah it is. Throw it away.

Dad: OK. But read this other one I got. Maybe it's legit.

Me: Throw it away Dad!!

Dad: Just read it. It sounds real.

Me: Here we go AGAIN!

☎
riga-luski and meatballs

Happens EVERY trash day when Dad cleans out his fridge.

Rrriiinnnggg

Me: Hello Dad.

Dad: Hey! Come over and get some stuffed cabbage, haluski, and macaroni that I have leftover.

Me: Thanks Dad, but why don't you keep it and just eat it for lunch or dinner tomorrow?

Dad: I don't have room in the refrigerator and I've had my fill.

Me: OK.

(Gather containers and…)

~ ~ ~ ~ *(Walk to Dad's.)* ~ ~ ~ ~

Dad: You don't need those containers. I have everything packed up. Why dirty your containers?

Me: Right!!! Experience tells me that I'm gonna want to use these containers.

Dad: Everything is packed up nice and tight in those two Walmart bags.

Me: Let me look.

—*Rigatoni packed in the tops of two Styrofoam takeout*

containers, taped together. He used the bottoms as cat dishes for a stray cat on his porch. No explanation as to why he would not just ruin one and leave one intact, choosing instead to render both useless.

—Spaghetti sauce in an empty half-gallon milk container with no lid.

—Stuffed cabbage in an empty butter tub with a too small, ill-fitting piece of what was once press and seal wrap.

—Meatballs in a red Solo cup with foil as a lid.

—A Dollar Store sandwich bag, non-zip-style, filled to the top with haluski.

Me: Dad, I'm gonna re-pack this so it doesn't spill. I have real containers with real lids.

Dad: Just take it. You coulda been home already. Just be careful.

~ ~ ~ ~ ~ *(Walk back home…being very careful…to no avail.)*

Tonight's dinner menu: Riga-luski and meatballs with UNstuffed cabbage, all of which spilled in the bags all over my unused REAL containers with REAL lids. Thanks Dad, it was delicious!!!

replacements and refills

Rrriiinnnggg

Me: Hello Dad! What's up?

Dad: I need some help putting up my Christmas lights.

Me: No problem. I'll be right over.

~ ~ ~ ~ *(Walk to Dad's.)* ~ ~ ~ ~

Me: OK, where are the lights?

Dad: In those bags, over there.

Me: Dad, there are thirty bags of lights? What are we decorating, 12th Street?

Dad: No, just my porch… but not all of those lights work.

Me: I spent three hours last year sorting out the good from the bad lights. I even threw out the broken ones. You saved them didn't you???

Dad: Well MAYBE I decided to take them back out of the trash and get replacement bulbs for the broken ones.

Me: Did you ever get replacement bulbs and fix the broken sets?

Dad: No. But I meant to.

Me: Well did you at least keep the broken strands separate from the working sets when you put them away?

Dad: No, but that is an excellent idea for this year.

Me: No Dad. I'm taking the broken strands and throwing them away in MY trash so that this doesn't happen again next year.

Dad: Just start checking the strands. I'll keep the broken ones separate, fix them and donate them to Goodwill for folks in need.

[How can you argue with that charitable attitude?]

√ √ √ √ √ √ √ √ … *We check thirty sets of lights.*

Me: OK Dad, these three sets work. I'll put these up on the porch. But first I want to mark those bags of "bad" lights so that we don't go through this again. Where are your pens?

Dad: On the table by the phone, in a cup.

Me: *(Retrieving pen)* Dad, you've got forty-five pens in this cup and none of them work. Why do you keep them?

Dad: I was going to buy refills for them.

Me: Did you buy refills?

Dad: No, but I meant to. I did buy a new pen though.

Tony Vavlas

Me: OK, where is the new pen?

Dad: It's mixed in with those.

Me: This is like ink pen Russian roulette.

Dad: You have NO patience.

Me: Can we throw away the "dead" pens?

Dad: Yes, but throw them away at your house. I can't be trusted.

Me: Am I adopted?

talk radio

Me: Hey Dad, I came over today and you weren't home but the radio was blaring. I could hear it loud and clear.

Dad: I heard on the news that it's a good security tactic. It scares away potential burglars.

Me: While I might agree, I don't think Dan Fogelberg and Soft Hits of the 70s is scaring away anybody. In fact I think that roughly translates to "come beat me up and take all my stuff" in burglar language. Maybe switch to talk radio, that Rush Limbaugh scares everybody.

Dad: You might be right.

wise men

Rrriiinnnggg

Me: Hello Dad.

Dad: Do you have the three wise men from my manger set?

Me: No. Do you need me to come and help you look for them.

Dad: No. I'll figure something out.

(Later at Dad's.)

Me: Did you ever find the wise men?

Dad: No but I fixed it.

Me: Really Dad??? Han Solo, C3-PO, and a Stormtrooper action figures as the three wise men?

Dad: Merry Christmas and May the Force be with you!!!

☎

food safety

Rrriiinnnggg

Me: Hello Dad.

Dad: Hey! I left half of a leftover chicken sandwich from a restaurant in my car overnight. Is it safe to eat?

Me: No!!!

Dad: But it was cold last night.

Me: Not cold enough.

Dad: It was 30 degrees.

Me: But your car is in a garage and sealed up with closed windows. The temp never got that cold in your car.

Dad: I'm sure that it did.

Me: I'm sure that it didn't. You know all of those half full water bottles in your back seat?

Dad: Yeah…

Me: Are they frozen?

Tony Vavlas

Dad: No.

Me: See, the temp never got below 32 degrees. It probably stayed above 40 degrees. Germs party above 40 degrees and invite all of their friends.

Dad: So it's not safe? Are you sure?

Me: It might be safe but not worth chancing it!!!

Dad: I think it's safe!

Me: Then why did you call me to ask?

Dad: Because I thought you'd reassure me that it was OK. I didn't think you'd be this unreasonable.

Me: I'm not gonna lie to you.

Dad: In this case, I wouldn't have minded.

Me: Listen, would you go to a restaurant where the cook left food in his car all night and then served it to people the next day?

Dad: What kind of car does he have?

Me: It doesn't matter, that's NOT the important part.

Dad: Well I just wondered what kind of car he might have.

Me: I guarantee you he isn't driving a Frigidaire!!!

Dad: So what should I do?

Me: Throw out the sandwich and eat something else!!!

Dad: Would it have mattered if I had left my windows down?

Me: NO!!! It's a car, not a walk in cooler. Does Toyota have an ice maker option?

<<<CLICK.>>>

the spy

Rrriiinnnggg

Me: Hello Dad, what's up.

Dad: Shhhhhhh…

Me: What??? What's the mat—*(interrupted by Dad)*

Dad: Listen…

Me: What am I listening for?

Dad: Shhhhhhh… Can you hear that guy talking???

Me: The crazy one who calls me a couple of times a day??? Yeah!!!

Dad: Shhhhhhhh… NO!!! The hillbilly guy. I can always hear him when I'm on the phone with somebody.

Me: Great!!! Voices. And what do these voices tell you to do? Did they tell you to call me?

Dad: It's not voices, it's one guy and I always hear him when I'm on the phone.

Me: Well, your cordless phone is from the 70s. It's probably picking up CB traffic from the turnpike. Try lowering the antenna on the handset about a foot and a half or so.

Dad: Maybe somebody is spying on me.

Me: A hillbilly guy who talks when he should be listening? He's a spy?

Dad: I didn't say he was a good spy.

Me: Why would anybody spy on you?

Dad: Maybe to find out when I'm not going to be at home.

Me: So you think that's this guy's plan?

Tony Vavlas

Dad: You aren't taking this serious. I don't like people knowing everything I say on the phone!

Me: Yeah, that would be terrible. I wonder if he posts your conversations on the internet?

Dad: Shhhhhh… There he goes again.

Me: Alright Dad, I gotta get back to work. Keep me posted on Double Wide O-7 the spy.

Dad: Shhhhhhh…

☎
why didn't you just say melted?

Rrriiinnnggg

Me: Hello Father.

Dad: Yeah… Hi. What temperature is ham supposed to be again?

Me: 165 degrees internal. And the fat should be rendered somewhat.

Dad: Tender?

Me: No rendered.

Dad: What in the hell does that mean? Do I need special equipment for that?

Me: Uhhhhhh, no!!! An oven should do. It means heated until it melts.

Dad: Oh, that's better. Why didn't you just say melted?

Me: Why are you cooking a ham?

Dad: I cooked my Christmas ham.

Me: Wow! I thought your 9 am Thanksgiving Day turkey was early but to have a Christmas ham done on the 21st, you've outdone yourself.

Dad: In case I get company before Christmas.

Me: Christmas company before Christmas Eve doesn't deserve Christmas ham. Besides, who's gonna visit you before Christmas?

Dad: I don't know, somebody might stop over. Aren't you coming over tomorrow?

Me: Yeah, to watch the BROWNS game but that hardly warrants a Holiday ham!

Dad: You better eat some ham. I made a whole ham and it better not go to waste.

Me: How did this ham become my problem?

Dad: Can I make ham and bean soup with some of it? Will you eat ham and bean soup tomorrow during the game?

Me: Whoooooooooa!!! You just made a Christmas ham on December 21st and you are already turning it into ham and bean soup on the 22nd? Three days BEFORE Christmas!?! Slow down… RELAX!!! It'll all be OK.

Dad: Oh brother… I gotta go. You make my nerves RENDERED!!! Come over and get a ham sandwich!

<<<<CLICK.>>>

evel knievel's glasses

Rrriiinnnggg

Me: Hello Dad.

Dad: I'm not going back to [Unnamed National Vision and Eyeglass store] again. I've had to take my glasses back twice already to be fixed.

Me: Dad!!! The first time was because you dropped them in a parking lot and then ran them over with your buggy. The second time you left them on your car seat and Joe sat on them. Both times the glasses were shattered and they covered the damage under your "scratched lens coverage". How do you figure it's their fault?

Dad: Those glasses are obviously cheaply made if they fall apart at the slightest touch.

Me: Slightest touch? Evel Knievel took better care of his glasses than you do.

Dad: They should make them better.

Me: They should bolt them to your head.

Dad: Can't you ever just be on my side???

ask

Me: Dad, give it up already!!! Mrs. T's is NEVER gonna make a lekvar pierogi. And no amount of complaining to the store manager is ever gonna change that!

Dad: You never get anything... unless you ask.

sexy tree

The following happened a few Christmases ago while my dear Mom was still with us.

Me: Hey Mom, did you let Dad set up the tree unsupervised?

Mom: Yeah, why?

Me: I think he's got sections two and three reversed.

Mom: I thought it looked strange.

Me: Haha... your tree has an hourglass figure.

Dad: Shut up! You're just jealous because my tree is sexier than your tree.

☎
harold's angels

A few Christmas Eves ago...

Dad: *(Singing in church)* Hark as Harold's Angels sing... Glory to the newborn King.

Me: *(Whispering at song's end)* Harold's Angels???

Dad: Yes.

...

Dad: Shut up... you're lucky we're in church!!!

☎
lionel richie

OK. I set my Dad up with an internet account and, because he can't type very well, I taught him how to use Google Voice Search. Our last phone call went like this.

Rrriiinnnggg

Me: Hello.

Dad: Hey Ton, this Google thing is broken. No matter what I search for it brings up Lionel Richie.

Me: What do you mean it keeps bringing up Lionel Richie? What are you doing?

Dad: I click on the button... like you told me... and then I say HELLO. Before I can say anything else... poof... it's Lionel Richie.

Me: Stop saying "HELLO" first when it asks you to say what you are searching for. You don't have to be polite. HELLO is a Lionel Richie song. THAT is why you keep getting Lionel Richie.

Dad: This Google thingy listens worse than you do!!!

Tony Vavlas

really tired

Last New Years Eve… at 9 PM

Rrriiinnnggg

Me: Hello Dad.

Dad: Happy New Year!!!

Me: Happy New Year Dad but you're a LITTLE early. Aren't you coming over?

Dad: NO!!! I'm going to bed! Happy Birthday too. I'm really tired. I might not be up by July 22nd.

not emergencies

Rrriiinnnggg… at 6:30 AM on NEW YEAR'S DAY!!!

Me: Hello Dad! This better be an emergency!

Dad: It is. I turned on my computer this morning to play my card games and an ad popped up telling me I could get internet for $19.99 per month. Then another ad popped up for anti-virus something something.

Me: OK. Happy New Year Dad. Those are NOT emergencies! Right now you get FREE internet piggybacking off of my signal and you already have anti-virus software installed. I took care of that when you got the computer.

Dad: So I should ignore them?

Me: YES!! They are called pop up ads. They are the internet version of junk mail. Unless you want to pay for internet and overprotect your computer then just click off of them.

Dad: I don't know what to do. I'll just leave them on the screen. Can you come over to look at them?

Me: Not right NOW!!! It's not even light outside yet!

Dad: But you're up.

Me: Because you called me.

Dad: Then why did you answer if you were sleeping?

Me: Because when someone calls you very, very early it's usually some type of emergency.

Dad: It is an emergency. I want to play solitaire.

Me: You have a deck of cards in the kitchen drawer.

Dad: It's not the same. I like the sound the game makes when all of the cards flip on the screen.

Me: Just X-out of those ads. They aren't important.

Dad: Are you sure? I'll just leave them on the screen until you come over later… maybe in about an hour?

Me: OK. I'm going back to sleep now. Did you need anything else Dad?

Dad: Yeah… my pork roast is done. Do you want any??

shakira, part 2

Rrriiinnnggg

Me: Hello Dad.

Dad: Hey! Did you send me *US* magazine?

Me: No. I ordered you *Crazy Old Man Illustrated*… did they mess it up??? No, I didn't order you *US* magazine.

Dad: Well somebody DID! I got one yesterday, and it's addressed to me.

Me: Dad, I've told you, when you order those Ginsu Can Openers

Tony Vavlas

or Amish Electric Heaters and stuff like that on TV, they sell your name to everybody. Magazine companies will send you a few "sample issues" and then send you a bill asking you to start paying to keep the magazines coming. They are hoping that you like what you see and want to continue getting it.

Dad: Well… I don't want it. Who do I call to get it to stop.

Me: You don't have to call anybody. Just throw away the bill when it comes and they'll eventually stop sending the magazine.

3 hours later… *Rrriiinnnggg*

Me: Hello Dad.

Dad: I found a 1-800 number in the magazine for subscriptions. I called them and told them to stop sending them. They had me on hold forever.

Me: Dad, the SAME THING could have been accomplished if you didn't do anything.

Dad: Well I was afraid that they'd accidentally charge me.

Me: Were you afraid that you'd accidentally PAY IT??

Dad: No, but peace of mind is a good thing. Do you think I should send back the issue that I got?

Me: No Dad, just enjoy it as they intended.

Dad: OK. Goodbye.

2 hours later… *Rrriiinnnggg*

Me: Hello Dad.

Dad: There was an article about Shakira in the magazine. Is she in there a lot?

Me: Probably. It's a celebrity gossip magazine and she's a gossipy celebrity.

Dad: Maybe I should have let them send a few more free issues to find out if I like their magazine or not.

Me: Yep… Maybe!

Dad: Do you think I can call the 1-800 number again and tell them that I changed my mind?

Me: Probably NOT!

Dad: Dang! I might just call and subscribe to *US* magazine then.

Me: Hahaha… Somehow they got EXACTLY what they wanted out of you and didn't have to use any bait. It's a good thing you aren't a fish, there'd be tartar sauce in your very near future!!! But enjoy your peace of mind.

Dad: <<<***CLICK.***>>>

room temperature

Rrriiinnnggg

Me: Hello Dad.

Dad: Hey! This recipe calls for room temperature milk. What does that mean? Any room??

Me: No Dad, it usually means a study, den, or conservatory.

Dad: A what? I don't have those rooms.

Me: I guess you can't make that recipe then. Sorry, I bet it would have been good. What were you making anyway?

Dad: Galaktoboureko [a Greek pastry].

Me: Oh! That would be fine. Greek recipe milk can be the temperature of almost any room in the house. Just so that the milk isn't chilled at all. It should be the same temperature as the kitchen.

Dad: You're an idiot!!!

<<<***CLICK.***>>>

Tony Vavlas

(ten minutes later I realize that I may have given him BAD info)

Rrriiinnnggg

Dad: Hello.

Me: Hey! Room temperature means the temperature of a NORMAL person's room. Usually 68 to 72 degrees, NOT the 95 degrees that you normally keep your house at in winter!!

Dad: Thanks… and you're still an idiot.

act now

Rrriiinnnggg

Me: Hello Dad.

Dad: Hi. I ordered us a NuWave Oven.

Me: You said that last time and it was the NuWave Cooktop that needs special pans to make it work.

Dad: Well this time it IS the oven.

Me: What's wrong with your regular oven.

Dad: Nothing but this one cooks in ¼ the time. It cooks a chicken in twenty minutes.

Me: Oh great, now your dinner will be ready at 4:30 am instead of 9 am!!!

Dad: Or I can sleep later, start it later, and call you later to tell you if it's done.

Me: I like it already!!!

Dad: It also comes with a Twister Blender.

Me: What in the heck is that?

Dad: It's a blender and a juicer.

Me: Oh, like the Magic Bullet that you bought… the LAST blender you will ever need. So why do you need a Twister? Someone lied to you.

Dad: Shut up! And I acted now so they upgraded me to the PROFESSIONAL one.

Me: You acted NOW? The commercial was on LIVE television?

Dad: Uhhh, I don't know but they told me to act now to be upgraded to the PRO model. So I did.

Me: The PROFESSIONAL MODEL??? I've worked in a lot of commercial kitchens and I can surely tell you that I've never used any equipment that was sold on TV between episodes of *Green Acres.*

Dad: Well, the pro model didn't cost any more, because I acted NOW!

Me: Good Job Dad!!! I can hardly wait. In three to six weeks we will be enjoying twenty-minute baked chicken and washing it down with nutritious fruit and vegetable juice.

Dad: You wait and see, this is gonna be great!

Me: Just like all of the other "As seen on TV" stuff you've bought! Your house looks like Ron Popeil's warehouse.

Dad: Ron who??

Me: The guy who sold you that crappy Pocket Fisherman and Ronco Pasta Maker!

Dad: This is gonna be different. And I got a second one free just for paying separate shipping and handling.

Me: Yeah… They are shipping and you got handled.

nevermind

Rrriiinnnggg

Tony Vavlas

Me: Hey Dad. I made homemade wild rice and mushroom soup today and jalapeño cornbread. Do you want some?

Dad: Sure!

(I spend twenty minutes packing it up.)

~ ~ ~ ~ *(I walk it over to Dad's.)* ~ ~ ~ ~

Dad: *(Takes one look)* Never mind. I don't like mushrooms, or wild rice or jalapeños or cornbread. What else you got?

Me: A headache!!!

☎

dr. doolittle

Dad is plagued by a nasty cold and sore throat so I thought I'd call him to see if he needed anything.

Rrriiinnnggg

Dad: Hello.

Me: Hey Dad, it's me. Are you feeling any better? Do you need anything from the store?

Dad: I'm about the same. What store are you at?

Me: I'm at Giant Eagle.

Dad: I need one package of iced oatmeal cookies and one package of un-iced oatmeal cookies.

Me: OK. Anything else?

Dad: Wait, Giant Eagle? Are you going to the Dollar Store?

Me: I can. What do you need from there?

Dad: The oatmeal cookies.

Me: They have those here.

Dad: But I don't think they will eat them from there. They like them from the Dollar Store.

Me: They? Who are "they?"

Dad: My squirrels.

Me: The cookies are for your squirrels? I'm not worried about THEM. I asked if YOU needed anything.

Dad: All I need is those cookies. But I don't think they'll eat the ones from Giant Eagle.

Me: Should I hold on while you ask them?

Dad: Are the oatmeal cookies good from there?

Me: Yes, they're very good. And I think they're even PETA approved.

Dad: Who's Peter?

Me: Oh Boy!!! Do you want me to buy these or not?

Dad: You're not going to the Dollar Store?

Me: I wasn't… but I guess I can. Is there anything else that YOU need?

Dad: Are you going to Marc's?

Me: I have a sneaking suspicion that I am NOW!! What do you need?

Dad: Birdseed. The one with the dried fruit mixed in.

Me: OK! Got it!!! Do you need anything else Dr. Doolittle?

Dad: Not unless you are going to Walmart.

Me: Did I mention that I am at GIANT EAGLE right now???

Dad: Never mind.

Me: What do you need from Walmart?

Tony Vavlas

Dad: Cat food.

Me: OK. I was hoping this would be a quick call to see if you needed any help, being that you are sick, and NOT turn into a wild goose chase. I'll see you around midnight.

Dad: Oh yeah!!! Wild goose. I need some crackers to feed the geese at the park.

Me: Can I buy those at Giant Eagle?

Dad: Sure, geese aren't picky like squirrels.

aurora borealis

Rrriiinnnggg

Me: Hey Dad, they say if you look to the northeast tonight, you can see the Aurora Borealis.

Dad: Aurora Borealis??? Who the hell is that? A Greek stripper at the Palace Bar?

snow beast

Rrriiinnnggg

Dad: What's up?

Me: Can you open the garage so that I can get the snow blower out?

Dad: Are you going to use the big one?

Me: The "BEAST?" No! No WAY!!! I just want the normal snow blower so that I can get this done quickly. I'll do yours, mine, and then help out a couple of the neighbors. It's too cold out here to monkey around with that Army surplus tank/snow machine today.

Dad: Well it needs to be started up to see if it still runs.

Me: Not today! It's too cold to play around. I just want to get this DONE!!!

Dad: Wait, I'll come out and help.

Me: Oh great, I didn't have any other plans today. I'd love to turn a one hour job into a three day project.

(Dad fills the tank with gas.)

Dad: Shut up and pull the cord.

<<<Tuuuuuuuuuuug!>>>

Me: Nothin'!

Dad: Did you prime it?

Me: Yes six times, no more, no less—as you've instructed me to do on every piece of equipment I've ever operated for as long as I can remember.

Dad: You must've messed up and did it seven times. You flooded it. Where's the ether? Get me the ether!!

Me: OK. Where do you keep your 1950s hospital operating room?

Dad: What?!? Ether, get me the ether...

Me: Let's see... leaches, eye of newt, Mercurochrome... no ether here doctor!

Dad: Starting fluid, get me the starting fluid.

Me: Oh!!!

Dad: OK, when I spray, you pull.

Me: OK.

<<<Tuuuuuuuuuuuug—baaaaaannnnnggggg!>>>

Tony Vavlas

<<<Up goes a large puff of black smoke.>>>

Me: I'll be damned, it's running.

Dad: OK, let it warm up for about twenty minutes before you engage the auger and treads.

Me: Dad!!! I could be done in twenty minutes with the other one.

Dad: No!! Use this one, it's better. It takes a bigger bite.

(Twenty minutes later, I engage the auger and treads. It rips a large piece of asphalt out of the driveway and dies.)

Me: I think you have it set to rototill. That'll be useful in May. Now can I use the normal snow blower that didn't see any action in WWII?

Dad: It just needs a final delicate adjustment.

Me: Yeah, with a car crusher at the junkyard.

Dad: *(Making adjustments)* OK… try it now.

<<<Tuuuuuuuuug… cord snaps!>>>

Me: I don't think that worked.

Dad: OK, just use the other one. But it needs gas.

Me: OK. Hey!!! This can is empty.

Dad: I know. I put five gallons in the BEAST!!!

Me: That's OK. I'll go and get my gas can.

Dad: That WAS your gas can. I borrowed it one day. Holly left your garage open. I always tell you to keep your garage closed… somebody's gonna steal something.

Me: I never thought it would be my own Father!!!

(3½ hours later… the driveways are done!!!)

☎
a bad feeling

Rrriiinnnggg

Me: Hello.

Dad: I have a problem

Me: Well, admitting it is half the battle. What's wrong?

Dad: I bought cat litter and bought the multi-cat kind by mistake.

Me: What's the problem?

Dad: I only have one cat. Will this litter be OK?

Me: Well, the way I see it, you really only have two options. 1) Get a second cat or 2) Start doing your business in the box too?

Dad: Really??? Why don't you bring one of your cats over to use the litter box.

Me: No Dad, it will be fine. My cats don't play well on "away games." Your cat won't even know the difference.

Dad: I have a better idea. Because you have more than one cat. You come over and take this and then go buy me the right kind at the store.

Me: It's 11 degrees without the windchill, the roads are icy and snow covered, AND you have a twenty-five pound bag of PERFECTLY GOOD cat litter right now.

Dad: But this is multi-cat.

Me: It doesn't matter. She can't read. She'll never know.

Dad: She'll know.

Me: That cat is bipolar anyways. Her multiple personalities more that make up for the fact that she's one cat.

Tony Vavlas

Dad: OK. I'll try this but if it doesn't work, I'm gonna need you to go to the store.

Me: OK. You stay on "box watch" all day and report back to me tomorrow... AFTER 7 am. I'll be sleeping in. I'm off tomorrow.

Dad: I have a bad feeling about this.

Me: Me too... me TOO!!!

☎
the right green

Sitting at a red light... Dad in the passenger seat.

The light changes to green as I am searching through radio stations.

Dad: Was there a particular shade of green that you're waiting for?

☎
ginger ale

Went with Dad to the grocery store... stopped for a sandwich first...

Counter Girl: Would you like something to drink with your order?

Dad: I'll have a ginger ale.

Counter Girl: I'm sorry, we don't carry ginger ale. We have Pepsi products.

Dad: Well you should tell your manager that older folks like ginger ale.

Me: OK Dad, she's not gonna be able to get it right now. He'll have a Pepsi.

Counter Girl: Thank you.

(She retreats to gather our order.)

Dad: I can't believe that they don't have ginger ale!!! Whenever I go for procedures at the hospital they give me a ginger ale and crackers when I wake up. It's good stuff.

Me: Did she ask you to disrobe to the waist, make you lie on a paper sheet, and stick a camera up your butt?

Dad: No, no and NO!

Me: Then why in the world would you think that she has any ginger ale back there? This is a fast food place. They carry what MOST people want! Besides, anything tastes good after you wake up at the doctor's.

Dad: A lot of folks like ginger ale.

Me: I know, just like the tapioca pudding you asked for last time we stopped to eat!

Counter Girl: *(returns with order)* Here you go.

Dad: Did you tell your manager???

Me: *(((Nodding furiously behind Dad's back)))*

Counter Girl: Uhhhh… yes sir.

Dad: See! Maybe they'll have ginger ale the next time we're here. Thank you honey!

(Later at the grocery store…)

Dad: What's that?

Me: It's ginger ale. I'm getting you a case. You seem to be craving it.

Dad: Eh!! Forget it! The moment's passed! I'm over it!!! But I do want tapioca pudding now that you mentioned it!

seeking mr. al capella

Rrriiinnnggg

Tony Vavlas

Me: Hello.

Dad: Hey. I have a question for you.

Me: OK

Dad: Who is Al Capella?

Me: I have no idea. But I'm working now. Can I call you back later?

Dad: OK.

(((An hour later...)))

Rrriiinnnggg

Me: Did you figure out who Al Capella is? Is it someone you worked with?

Dad: No. I was watching TV, flipping through the channels and I saw a singing group on PBS singing doo wop and they were really good. The info guide said it was Al Capella's group so I figured he was a record producer or singer.

Me: Singing?

Dad: Yeah.

Me: Any chance it said A Capella groups instead of Al Capella's group? Were they singing without music?

Dad: Yes they were. Well... that would make more sense now, wouldn't it?

Me: Maybe just a little.

yolo

Rrriiinnnggg

(I was talking to my Dad about the prospect of me buying and

operating a food truck.)

Dad: I think it's a good idea… after all… YOLO.

Me: Did you just say YOLO???

Dad: Yeah, I heard it on Steve Harvey. I think it's African.

Me: No Dad, it most definitely isn't.

Dad: It means "you're only young once."

Me: No, it means "you only live once."

Dad: I think you're wrong on this one… it's "you're only young once."

Me: No Dad… that would be YOYO. Spell it out with the letters.

Dad: Why don't you Gooble it?

Me: GOOGLE! Of all the things you could have learned on TV today, YOLO is what you came away with?

Dad: Well it fits in this situation. I think you should do it if that's what you want to do… while you're still young! YOLO!!!

Me: Every time you say YOLO it takes a year off of my life!

no visitors

Rrriiinnnggg

Me: Hello.

Dad: You know… I'm getting older.

Me: I've noticed… but isn't that the point in life?

Dad: What if, at some point, I become too much for you to handle?

Me: What do you mean "if?" and "at some point?" You mean you could get harder to handle than you are right now?

Tony Vavlas

Dad: Ha Ha! Very funny. I mean what if you have to put me in a nursing home some day. Do you know what to look for in a good home?

Me: Yes. Top notch medical care, good food, a warm and friendly atmosphere, and a written promise that they won't allow you access to a telephone!

Dad: You're a real jerk! Make sure they don't allow visitors as well! And I'm going to need a safe in my room to store my will... AFTER I REWRITE IT!!!

☎
mean and greedy

Rrriiinnnggg

Dad: Hello.

Me: Hey!!! I'll be over in fifteen minutes to shovel your driveway and walks.

Dad: OK... I'm gonna go out now and do the front steps and walk though.

Me: OK??? Can't it wait fifteen minutes?

Dad: No! I want to get it cleared off for the squirrel.

Me: Oh, of course. What was I thinking? The squirrel absolutely needs IMMEDIATE access to your porch! Why don't you just let him in your house and give him some soup?

Dad: Because I don't think him and Angel [the cat] would get along.

Me: Really??!!?? I mean REALLY??!!?? THAT'S the ONLY reason you can think of to NOT let a squirrel into your house???

Dad: Well... THAT and then he'd want to invite his friends the blue jays in and those suckers are mean and greedy.

Me: Good call Dad!! Good call!!

lopsided

Dad: How'd your eye appointment go?

Me: Well, I'm nearsighted and farsighted.

Dad: And a little bit lopsided.

thin excuses

Rrriiinnnggg

Dad: Will you take this trash bag out?

Me: Sure… wait, it's leaking. Give me another bag.

Dad: Don't waste another bag. Put tape over the hole.

Me: I'm not going to repair a trash bag that you got for free. It's just a Walmart bag. You have 7,000 of them under the sink. Just give me another one to double bag this one.

Dad: That's wasteful… move, I'll tape it.

(((The bag rips, trash spills onto floor. I clean it up and put it into the Walmart bag that I asked for in the first place.)))

Me: See!!! Now we wasted paper towels and cleaner to clean this up and still ended up using the bag that I asked for in the first place!!!

Dad: This wouldn't have happened if you would have just taped the bag when I asked you instead of arguing with me.

Me: Your excuse is thinner than that bag!!!

three dollars

Rrriiinnnggg [Dad's Cell]

Tony Vavlas

Me: Hello.

Dad: Help!!! I'm locked out of my house. My key won't turn. I think it's frozen.

Me: I'll be right over.

~ ~ ~ ~ ~ (Walk to Dad's.) ~ ~ ~ ~ ~

Me: Let me see your key.

Dad: Here.

Me: What the heck is this attached to your key?

Dad: A light, so I can see the keyhole.

Me: Well, the lock's not frozen. This light isn't allowing the key to go in all of the way. It has to come off.

Dad: But it was $1.48 at Walmart and I need it to see the keyhole.

Me: Well, you've got two choices. See the keyhole and stand out here and freeze, or remove the light and open the door with the key. Which one is it gonna be?

Dad: Can't you move the light higher?

Me: It's a key. Not a lot of wiggle room on a key.

Dad: But it was $1.48.

Me: Right now I'll give you $3 if you let me remove it so we can unlock the door. It's cold out here.

Dad: Hmmmmm…

Me: Give me the key again.

\\\I remove the light, reposition it on an unused key on the key ring, and UNLOCK THE DOOR.

Me: THERE!!! Problem solved.

Dad: Thanks.

Me: You're welcome. I'll talk to you later.

Dad: Aren't you forgetting something?

Me: What?

Dad: You owe me $3

☎
i wish i had your thighs

Rrriiinnnggg

Me: Hello.

Dad: Hey! I got these breasts and I don't like them. I wish I had your thighs.

Me: What?!?!

Dad: I bought you fried chicken and me fried chicken and I don't like the white meat. I want to trade them for the thighs in your box.

Me: Haha… you probably shoulda started with… "I bought us some fried chicken."

☎
reasonable lunch

Rrriiinnnggg

Holly: Hello.

Grandpa [My Dad]: Hey Holz… what time are we going to lunch tomorrow.

Holly: I get done with school at 11:30… how about 12 noon?

Grandpa: 12 noon? I thought we were going to lunch?

Holly: 12 noon IS LUNCH!!!

Grandpa: No! 10:30 is lunch. You live just like your father.

Tony Vavlas

Holly: Reasonably?!?!? Haha!

Grandpa: Very funny. OK… 12 noon it is. It'll give me a chance to recover from watching Shakira on Good Morning America.

Holly: Maybe we better make it dinner then!

Grandpa: 12 noon IS DINNER. I'll see you then.

☎
shakira, part 3

Rrriiinnnggg

Me: Hello.

Dad: It's almost time!!!

Me: OK, I'll call Wasko's Funeral Home. You've been a good Dad.

Dad: Noooo dummy! I feel fine. It's almost SHAKIRA time! On TV.

Me: Oh! It still might be a good idea to keep Wasko's number handy while you're watching though.

☎
next time

I took my Dad to dinner tonight and I had the audacity to try to pay.

Dad: *(to cashier)* He's using a stolen bank card.

Cashier: I have to keep this card.

Me: You know he's kidding, right?

Cashier: I don't know that. Do you have ID?

Me: I do. In the car. Do I really need to go and get it? Tell them you're kidding Dad.

Dad: Here… just take cash.

Me: No! I said I'm paying. Don't do anything with that check. I'll be right back.

///*I prove my identity.*///

Cashier: Sorry about that. Here are some coupons.

Me: Do you see this man's face. Remember it. He's crazy. Just in case I bring him here again. Which is doubtful.

Dad: Oh look… coupons for next time.

Me: There's not gonna be any next time.

☎

research

Dad wanted to try the new Chinese Buffet in the Boardman Plaza, so we went…

Me: *(After dinner)* So, what did you think?

Dad: It was OK?

Me: Just OK?

Dad: Yeah… there was a lot of stuff I didn't care for.

Me: Oh, but I see it took four plates of "research" to come to that conclusion.

Dad: Shut up! Are you in a hurry or can I go up for desserts?

Me: I have all night Dad.

Dad: Good… I might need to do some more research.

☎

emergency haircut

Rrriiinnnggg

Me: Hello.

Dad: Hey. Do you want to go get some pizza?

Me: I can't Dad. I'm working. And besides, it's only 10 am.

Dad: OK.

Rrriiinnnggg

Me: Hello.

Dad: Did you take my calendar?

Me: No Dad. Why would I take your calendar?

Rrriiinnnggg

Me: Hello.

Dad: I found my calendar.

Me: Haha… OK Dad. I'm trying to work. Please don't call me again unless it's an emergency or after 5 pm.

Dad: Jeez… Sorry!

(five minutes later...)

Rrriiinnnggg

Me: Hello.

Dad: I'm going to get a haircut.

Me: Really Dad?!?

Dad: Sorry… I'm going for an EMERGENCY haircut.

☎
elephant

Discussing the upcoming Cleveland Indians season with my Dad…

Dad: And let's not forget about the 400 pound elephant in the room. We haven't talked about the fact that they didn't add any bats in the off season.

Me: Forget about the bats. Where did they find such a tiny elephant and will he be appearing at home games for the kids to ride?

Dad: Shut Up!!!

☎
hipster

Dad, upon seeing a hipster with huge gauge earrings…

"That's gotta save space. He can sleep hanging from a curtain rod."

☎
mid-size madness

Rrriiinnnggg

Me: Hello.

Dad: Hey… Arby's is confusing.

Me: Not for most people. What happened?

Dad: They have a new sandwich called a "mid." It has more roast beef on it, and a "max" that has even more roast beef on it.

Me: Uhhhh, yeah. That is confusing. I hope they start teaching the Arby's menu in school or we are doomed, as a nation, to become a generation of folks who just pull up to the Arby's drive through, look at the menu, and weep.

Dad: Zip it! That's not the confusing part. It gets confusing because the "regular" roast beef should not be called regular. The mid-sized one should be the regular because that is the size the regular one was in the 60s.

Me: Well what do you think they should call the "regular" now? The "look how bad we're sticking it to you" size? All companies do that. They decrease the portion to keep the price lower.

Tony Vavlas

Dad: Well it's confusing. If you have a sandwich that is the size of a regular in the 1960s it should be called the regular today. Why would they do that to people?

Me: I blame the Soviets.

Dad: Huh? Well I explained it all to the manager but she didn't seem to care.

Me: That's probably because she wasn't even alive in the 1960s.

Dad: Well I took a comment card. I'm going to mail it in. I need you to help me get the wording right. Then you can mail it for me Monday.

Me: Uhhhh, sure.

Dad: You're not going to mail it are you?

Me: Probably not. It won't really make a difference.

Dad: I'll just mail it myself. Just come over and help me write it out.

Me: Are you sure that we can adequately describe your dilemma on a tiny comment card? Maybe you should just call them.

Dad: I already thought of that... I grabbed two cards.

Me: Good thinking Dad. When you go to the post office to mail it tomorrow make sure you pick up a few of their comment cards.

Dad: Why?

Me: Because the price of postage has gone up since the 1960s and the stamps aren't any bigger. That's confusing.

Dad: Shut up... <<<*CLICK.*>>>

crap! part 3

Happens every time...

Rrriiinnnggg

(Thirty seconds to find phone.)

(Thirty seconds to find glasses to read caller ID.)

(Forty-five seconds to find remote to turn down TV volume.)

Beeeeeeeeeeeep... answering machine.

Dad: Crap!!!! Missed another one.

cargo

Rrriiinnnggg

Me: Hello.

Dad: Hey, Are you off today?? Do you wanna go down to the casino?

Me: Sure. I'll be over in about twenty minutes.

~˜~˜~˜ *(Walk over to Dad's.)* ~˜~˜~˜

Me: Hey Dad... what in the heck are you wearing?

Dad: They're cargo shorts... like yours.

Me: Why do they look like they have the mumps? How much stuff do you have crammed in those pockets?

Dad: Uhhhhh... two pairs of eyeglasses... my sunglasses... my wallet... my pills... a snack pack of pretzels... a pack of cookies... a pen... a handkerchief... my eyedrops... an ace bandage in case my knee starts to hurt... some Tums... a water bottle... my Players Club card... and my GPS.

Me: Wow Dennis the Menace. No frog or slingshot?

Dad: Shut up, I got these shorts because of all of the pockets.

Me: But you didn't have to use all of them. We're not moving there, are we?

Dad: Zip it and get in the car.

(Dad gets in the car, then gets right back out.)

Dad: Crap!!! I forgot my phone.

Me: And the kitchen sink.

☎
leisurely weapon

Rrriiinnnggg

Me: Hello.

Dad: Did you put a chair in my yard?

Me: What???

Dad: Did you put that recliner out in front of my house.

Me: No. Why would I do that?

Dad: Why would you do most of the things you do?

Me: Thanks Dad. Do you want me to move it?

Dad: Maybe it belongs to somebody.

Me: You think it's a runaway? Is it on a leash? Does it have tags?

Dad: Shut up… should I call the police?

Me: For what? Assault with a leisurely weapon?

Dad: You're no help at all.

Me: I offered to move it.

Dad: It needs to go back to where it came from.

Me: Well then make sure you don't feed it. If you feed it then it will never go home.

Dad: <<<**CLICK.**>>>

☎
hanes

Rrriiinnnggg

Me: Hello.

Dad: Hey… what are you doing?

Me: I just sat down to eat dinner. What's up?

Dad: Can you come look at my leg? It hurts and there's a big lump on it.

Me: Did you bump it?

Dad: No… and it feels a little numb.

Me: I'll be right over!

~ ~ ~ ~ ~ *(Walk to Dad's.)* ~ ~ ~ ~ ~

Me: OK. Lemme see.

Dad: *(Pointing to a mark on his leg)* See the big lump?

Me: I don't see a lump. I see a mark on your leg from where your sock band was.

Dad: No. It's definitely a lump.

Me: I don't see it. You have the same mark on your other leg. What in the heck kind of socks were you wearing—tourniquets?

Dad: No, HANES… from the flea market.

Me: Well they're not the right size. They shouldn't mark your leg like that.

Dad: The socks fit fine. This is something medically wrong, like a blockage.

Me: No it's not. Your foot has good color, isn't numb, and isn't cold.

Dad: I think we should go to the ER.

Me: OK… let's go.

(((We arrive at the ER and sign in. Dad surveys the overcrowded waiting room.)))

Dad: I feel better. Let's go home.

Me: Nooooooo… we came here, we're gonna get that leg checked.

(((After a two hour wait to be seen, we are taken into triage.)))

Triage Nurse: So Anthony, what brings you to the ER tonight?

Dad: My son.

Nurse: No… I mean what is the reason for your visit?

Dad: Oh… we're not visiting anyone. We are here because my leg hurts. I think it's a blood cloth.

Nurse: What's a blood cloth?

Me: He means blood clot. Can you give him something for his speech impediment?

Nurse: Hahaha… Anthony, on a scale of one to ten where is your pain?

Dad: It's in my leg?

Me: I'm sorry ma'am.

Nurse: It's OK… I mean how severe is it?

Dad: About a two.

Me: But it's a SOLID two.

Nurse: OK… that's not too bad. Let me take a look.

(((She examines Dad's leg.)))

Nurse: Sir, what are these marks on your leg?

Me: They are from his socks. They don't fit.

Dad: They are HANES.

Me: From the flea market.

Nurse: Well I definitely wouldn't wear those any more. They are cutting off your circulation. That is more than likely the source of your pain but I'm going to put you in Urgent Care and have them order an ultrasound.

Dad: Is it a blockage?

Nurse: No… Your foot has good color, isn't numb, and isn't cold.

Me: Hmmmmmm… sound familiar?

(((Another 45 minute wait, followed by a 30 minute wait for the ultrasound.)))

Orderly: OK Anthony, I'm going to put you in room thirty-three while you wait for the results of your test.

Dad: Can you get me a tray?

Orderly: Uhhhh… errrrrr… I'm sorry sir. Those are for patients who have been admitted.

Dad: Can I be admitted?

Me: Sure… to the Psych Ward. I'll get you a bag of chips and a pop from the vending machine.

(((25 minutes later, the doctor arrives with ultrasound results.)))

Doctor: Anthony, the results of the ultrasound were negative.

Dad: *(to me)* See!!! I told you something was wrong!!!

Tony Vavlas

Me: Negative is GOOD Dad!!!

Doctor: He's right. Negative is GOOD. Let me see your leg.

(((He examines Dad's leg.)))

Doctor: Sir, what are these marks around your legs? Were you wearing tight socks?

Dad: They're HANES!!!

Me: From the flea market.

Doctor: Well Anthony… I'm going to recommend that you don't wear those again.

Dad: Should I buy diabetic socks?

Doctor: Are you diabetic?

Dad: No.

Doctor: Then NO, you should not buy diabetic socks. Just buy regular, normal, properly fitting socks.

Me: From a reputable retailer!!!

Doctor: YES!! From a reputable retailer. Avoid the flea market. I'm going to write you a prescription for a muscle relaxer and an anti-inflammatory.

Dad: And a meal tray?

Doctor: Haha… no, you're free to go home and eat anything you want.

Dad: Is it OK to take those pills on an empty stomach?

Me: When do you EVER have an empty stomach?

Dad: Shut up or your ass is gonna be at a seven on that pain scale.

☎

pedophiles

Dad… thumbing through the newest Penny Saver magazine.

Dad: Half of these coupons are for salons. What in the hell am I gonna do with those?

Me: Maybe you should go to one.

Dad: They're all buy one get one.

Me: Take Joe.

Dad: Yeah… we can go get pedophiles.

Me: You mean pedicures.

Dad: Whatever!!!

☎

crap! part 4

Rrriiinnnggg

Dad: Hello.

Me: Hey Dad. I left a bag of buttered popcorn flavored jelly beans in your car yesterday when we went to the store.

Dad: Oh, I asked a couple of my friends if they were theirs. They all said no. I couldn't figure out where they came from.

Me: No, they're mine. I'll be over in a minute to get them.

Dad: Oh… uhhhh… well… they're not here? They're gone.

Me: You ate a whole bag of jelly beans in less than 24 hours?

Dad: At first I tried one… they were good so I had a few more… then a few more and before I knew it… the bag was gone. I figured I would just buy you a new bag.

Tony Vavlas

Me: I thought you said you didn't know who they belonged to! Why were you planning to buy ME another bag.

Dad: Oh yeah… right. Crap.

☎
adopted

Shopping with Dad at Walmart…

Dad: Why are you buying THAT shampoo?

Me: Because I like it.

Dad: Should I buy some too?

Me: Uhhh… sure. You could. If you want.

Dad: Well what would you recommend for my hair?

Me: Elmer's Glue and holy water.

Dad: You're a real jerk!!! Did I ever tell you that you were adopted?

Me: No, but I always kinda felt like I didn't really fit in with this family.

Dad: Oh no! WE are your birth parents. We gave you up for adoption. A week later the adoptive parents begged us to take you back. And you know how your mother was. She felt bad.

Me: Thanks Dad. That's real nice. Maybe you better double up on the holy water. Lather. Rinse. Repent.

☎
tomato paper

Rrriiinnnggg

Me: Hello.

Dad: Hey… I bought you something off of TV. They were buy one get one.

Me: Hmmmmm… what is it this time?

Dad: It's a knife and it came with a free knife sharpener.

Me: The knife that you bought me last year was advertised as the last knife I'll ever need… and now I need ANOTHER one?

Dad: This one can cut through nails, shoes, a phone book, and even frozen vegetables… and it NEVER needs sharpening!

Me: Are you cutting a lot of nails, shoes, and books these days? You may need to change your diet.

Dad: Shut up! After all that it will still cut a tomato, paper thin.

Me: Wow!! A knife sharp enough to cut a tomato. We're probably gonna need special permits.

Dad: Just come get your knife… smartass!!!

Me: I have a question. If it never needs sharpening, why does it come with a free sharpener?

Dad: I wasn't looking for an interrogation. A simple thank you would have been nice.

Me: I was going to write you a thank you note as soon as I made some of that tomato paper.

<<<*CLICK.*>>>

empty

Rrriiinnnggg

Me: Hello.

Dad: What's goin' on?

Me: I don't know. I woke up with the room spinning again this morning. This vertigo won't go away.

Dad: Maybe it's just a spider. He probably crawled in your ear while you slept and he's eating your brain.

Me: Thanks Dad. I didn't have ENOUGH to worry about.

Dad: Don't worry he'll be out soon and he'll still be hungry. Poor little guy is probably running around your big empty head looking for crumbs.

☎
placenta

Rrriiinnnggg

Me: Hello.

Dad: Hey. Do you still have your recipe for placenta?

Me: Oh God, I hope you mean polenta. And if not… I hope my phone is not tapped.

☎
sock bird

Dad occasionally dog sits my neighbor Dave's dog.

Dad: (YELLING out his window to me as I barbecue) Hey!!! Ask Princess if she's ready to go inside.

Me: OK.

Dad: What did she say?

Me: She said "sock bird".

Dad: Sock bird???? What the hell does that mean?

Me: I don't know. I don't think she's as smart as other talking dogs.

Dad: Ask her again.

☎
john elway, cleveland antichrist

Rrriiinnnggg

Me: Hello.

Dad: You know what the problem is with the world today?

Me: We talked about this last week. I thought you decided it was interleague baseball.

Dad: That was last week. This week it's that Christianity has too many factions. Catholic, Protestant, Lutheran, Baptist…

Me: How is that so bad?

Dad: The devil has one team, Pure Evil. And we've got all of these other teams running around trying to beat him. Too many teams. It weakens the talent pool.

Me: Well think of Christianity as one team with one Head Coach… God. All of the branches of Christianity are like coordinators. All of them work for the same goal, to beat Satan.

Dad: Who would Jesus be?

Me: GM… I guess.

Dad: Well we better make some trades or get more aggressive on defense because every time I turn on the news, the devil is scoring more and more points. Breaking people's hearts. He's worse than John Elway. Well… almost.

surrender

Rrriiinnnggg

Me: Hello.

Dad: Hey… I cook this ham until the fat surrenders, right?

Tony Vavlas

Me: Haha… no, you want the fat to render—or melt—not surrender.

Dad: Well it's waving a white flag. I think it's done.

☎
barama / tavlas 2016

Rrriiinnnggg

Me: Hello.

Dad: Did you hear what Barama said about these air strikes?

Me: Come on Dad! He's been President for a term and a half now. Do you think it's time to stop calling him Oback Barama?

Dad: That's his name… right?

Me: No Dad, it's Barack Obama.

Dad: That's what I said… Oback Barama.

Me: Close but… No Dad. That would be like people calling you Vony Tavlas.

Dad: I like it. Kinda catchy.

☎
breakfast notes

Out to breakfast with Dad…

Server: Are you ready to order?

Dad: Yes. I'll have the steak and eggs.

Server: How do you want your eggs?

Dad: Over easy, scrambled.

Server: You want one of each?

Dad: No. Both the same way.

Me: That's two kinds of eggs Dad. Over easy is flipped but with a runny yolk, and scrambled is… uhhhhh… scrambled.

Dad: Well, I want them scrambled but over easy. Scrambled but not browned.

Me: He'll have them scrambled easy please.

Server: And how did you want your steak hon?

Me: Oh boy!!!

Dad: I want it well done but with a little pink.

Server: So medium-well then?

Dad: NO! I don't ever eat my steak medium anything. I like it well done… but with a little pink.

Me: THAT IS medium well Dad! Well done means no pink at all.

Dad: I don't think so. I don't eat medium steak… EVER!

Me: Trust me, it's what you want. He'll have the steak medium-well please.

Dad: *(pointing at me)* If it's bloody, you will be too.

Server: *(Laughing)* And what kind of toast?

Me: Here we go again!

Dad: Shut up! I'll have sourdough toast, dark but not burnt. I guess that's medium-well too then, huh?

Me: *(to server)* I'm sorry!

Dad: Why do I never have this trouble when you're not here?

Me: Because most servers are used to the incoherent babblings of customers and just order their food from the kitchen without trying to educate them. It's easier that way. I was trying to help you.

(((*The food arrives. Dad surveys his breakfast.*)))

Server: Does everything look good?

Dad: Perfect! Good job!!!

Me: See! Now you know how to order.

Dad: Well thanks for nothing! Thanks to you I'm gonna have to bring notes with me next time I go to breakfast.

☎

sunglasses

Rrriiinnnggg

Me: Hello.

Dad: Hey. I lost three pairs of sunglasses this week.

Me: I don't think there's a contest Dad... but if there was, my money's on you.

Dad: Come over and help me find them.

Me: OK. I'll be right over.

~ ~ ~ ~ *(Walk to Dad's.)* ~ ~ ~ ~

Me: Dad, here's a pair behind your TV. Has it been particularly sunny back there lately?

Dad: Shut up and keep looking.

Me: Here's another pair in your mailbox. I don't even know what to say about that.

Dad: I had two pairs with me so I put one pair in there for safe keeping. I figured I'd eventually check in there for mail and find them.

Me: Good thinking Dad. That's scary smart. Very scary.

Dad: Two down one to go.

Me: Sorry. I can't find the third pair.

Dad: Thanks for finding two.

((((Twenty minutes later…)))

Rrriiinnnggg

Me: Hello.

Dad: I found the third pair… in the shower.

Me: I don't even wanna know.

Dad: Even I don't know how they got in there.

too safe

Knock—knock // knock-knock—knock // knock—knock.

((((I get up to answer the door.)))

Dad: *(Frantically yelling)* Turn on the porch light. Check who it is.

((((I open door without checking. It's my daughter Holly)))

Dad: Are you goofy? It could have been burglars or murderers!!!

Me: Using Shave and a Haircut as their "secret" knock???

Dad: You can't be too safe!

making a point

Rrriiinnnggg (at 5:45 am on Saturday)

Me: Hello… this better be IMPORTANT!

Dad: It is. I'm cancelling the newspaper.

Tony Vavlas

Me: Oh! You might want to wait to see your name on the front page with the headline "Son files telephone harassment charges against father."

Dad: Shut up and listen! At least once a month they miss my porch and the paper lands on my driveway. I've had enough! I'm proving a point.

Me: Well you can't cancel the paper. You love to read the paper.

Dad: I'll just go to the store every day and buy one.

Me: So you will walk out of your house, down the steps, down the driveway—where once in a blue moon your paper lands—into your garage, drive to the store in all kinds of weather, and buy a paper at a higher price… just to prove a point? That sounds reasonable!

Dad: You may be right. Maybe I should just call and complain.

Me: If you call and complain, you'll reach somebody who will pretend to care, and pretend to be sorry, and pretend to write the issue down to be discussed at the next Board of Directors meeting. So do yourself a favor and save yourself some time by PRETENDING to call and complain. The poor paper carrier gets up in the middle of the night to deliver papers for very little compensation, to folks who are still sleeping comfortably in their beds. At that hour, you're lucky it's not just dropped at the curb.

Dad: It's not THAT early. I'm usually up when they deliver.

Me: Well you need to sleep later and stop calling me so early. My alarm clock is getting jealous.

Dad: What if I have them deliver the paper to your house and then you can bring it to me.

Me: Oh that's a great idea! I'd have a one person paper route and the customer is YOU! That would work fine as long as you don't mind evening delivery.

Dad: No… that's no good. I need to read it in the morning so that I can plan my day around whether or not I have to go to anybody's calling hours. Maybe I'll just wait on the porch and talk to the carrier myself and ask nicely to please get the paper onto my porch.

Me: OK. But do you remember when you asked the trash man "nicely" to not make so much noise in the middle of the night when he drove down our street? He squeezed the garbage juice out in front of our house for months! That was a rough smelling summer at 437 Whipple Ave!

Dad: But he did it quietly!

hackers

Rrriiinnnggg

Me: Hello.

Dad: I have an emergency... Is my cell phone safe?

Me: No phone is safe in YOUR hands and that's not an emergency.

Dad: I'm serious. Do I need to worry about hackers?

Me: What kinda crazy talk is that?

Dad: I heard on the news that a bunch of famous people had their phones hacked and had nude pictures of themselves stolen.

Me: Are you famous?

Dad: No.

Me: Do you have nude pictures of yourself on your cell phone?

Dad: Not that I know of.

Me: Were there any 71 year old men on the list of folks who got hacked?

Dad: Come to think of it... no!

Tony Vavlas

Me: Well then I think you are safe.

Dad: Is there anything I can do to make my phone safe from hackers?

Me: Maybe only use it in emergencies... REAL emergencies.

Dad: I'm being serious.

Me: I don't know, maybe wrap it in tinfoil.

Dad: That'll help?

Me: Can't hurt.

Dad: OK... thanks.

good job

Rrriiinnnggg

Me: Hello.

Dad: Hey... They threw me out of the doctor's office today. The head nurse said that I'm not allowed to come back.

Me: Oh God!!! Were you telling dirty jokes again or feeling up the nurses???

Dad: No... but I did kick cancer's ass and they only have time for sick patients.

Me: Good job Dad!!! Cancer never stood a chance.

Tony Vavlas is a first time author. Tony is a lifelong resident of Campbell, Ohio and lives there with his wife and daughter as well as one dog and four cats. Tony's father lives next door. Tony has been a son his entire life but has just recently taken on expanded duties. With the sudden passing of his Mom, Tony is tasked with fielding a multitude of phone calls on a variety of subjects from his Dad. The phone calls may occur at any and all hours of the day or night.

Some of Tony's other literary works include "Homework Stinks: A Study of Systematic Oppression within the American Educational System" in the 4th grade, for which he received a C+ and "Please Don't Turn Off the Lights, the Check is in the Mail" a letter to the Ohio Edison Power Company for which he received a late fee.

His hobbies include ghost hunting with his family and travelling. Tony also loves watching sporting events and routinely attends games with his Dad. Tony was raised (coerced) by his father to become a fan of all Cleveland sports franchises. It is a cross he bears proudly.

Tony is a graduate of Youngstown State University, receiving his degree after twenty-four years of study. It was there that Tony developed a love for writing and discovered his literary hero, Mike Royko. His freshman English professor compared Tony's work to that of his hero stating that "I cannot compare the quality of your work to that of Mr. Royko's, but it seems as though you use the same alphabet with somewhat less flair and efficiency."

Follow Tony on Facebook:
Facebook.com/You-Cant-Feed-Butter-to-a-Cat

☎
Books by 1701 Press
www.1701press.com

A is for Akron, an A to Z list of Akron's places and things that make us smile, by Karen Starr and Joanna Wilson
(2014, ISBN 978-0-9842699-2-1)

Merry Musical Christmas: Volume One, The Best Christmas Music in Television Sitcoms and Dramas, by Joanna Wilson
(2012, ISBN 978-09842699-0-7)

Tis the Season TV: the Encyclopedia of Christmas-Themed Episodes, Specials, and Made-for-TV Movies, by Joanna Wilson
(2011, ISBN 978-09842699-8-3)

The Christmas TV Companion: a Guide to Cult Classics, Strange Specials, and Outrageous Oddities, by Joanna Wilson
(2009, ISBN 978-09842699-4-5)

Made in the USA
Charleston, SC
22 January 2015